Creepy Kitchen

Creepy Kitchen

60 TERROR-RIFIC RECIPES THAT'LL POSSESS YOUR PALETTE

⚬⚬⚬ KIM KINDELSPERGER ⚬⚬⚬

Illustrations by Kitty Willow Wilson

ROCK
POINT

Contents

Introduction

Greetings, ghosts and goblins! When leaves turn yellow and days grow shorter, something magical happens: It becomes totally acceptable to buy too many decorative gourds. Three-foot spiders nestle into spider webs the size of a city bus. Jump scares are socially acceptable and even funny. It's the most wonderful, creepiest time of the year—Halloween. During this season, even the most ordinary meals can undergo a transformation, morphing into eerie delights that resemble jack-o'-lanterns, black cats, or skeletons. So, my dear friends, step into my Creepy Kitchen, where my personal creations will make your spine tingle and your stomach growl.

Spooktober, when I was a kid, was a time of wide-eyed wonder, candy-filled exhilaration, and face paint galore. I still remember the thrill of donning my favorite witch costume every year until it fell apart, the fun of taping pumpkin pictures to the front door, and wielding a knife for pumpkin carving. But it wasn't just about dressing up and decorations; it was the television shows, movies, and stories that introduced me to haunted mansions, headless horsemen, and *The Great Pumpkin*. These were tales I could revisit and enjoy at any time, thus keeping creep alive well beyond October. This marked the beginning of a lifelong enjoyment of all things dark and dreary, some of which I've shared on these pages.

Now, as an adult, I've embraced the macabre with open zombie arms and brought it into my kitchen. I love making dinners and dishes that are not only delicious but also delightfully curious, no matter what time of year it is. These recipes are not just for getting food on the table; they're playful reminders that food is fun and monsters are funny.

The other eleven months of the year need not lack weird and wonderful. Creepmas and Goth Valentine's Day are excellent opportunities to spread more doom and gloom into holiday fun. From fearsome Christmas legends to timeless tales of heartbreak, I've carefully curated recipes and lore that might make you shiver amid holiday cheer and will definitely help you create unforgettable get-togethers, one spooky dish at a time.

Within these pages, you'll find a mixture of quick and easy homemade creations and monstrous makeovers of ready-made, store-bought items. Fear not, there are also dishes that invite you to linger in the kitchen for a spell, to savor the process of a full-fledged incantation. You'll find suggestions for weeknight meals, last-minute school parties, and coven get-togethers that are sure to be the talk of the supernatural town.

I've poured my tell-tale heart and pilfered soul into this cookbook, and I hope you find it as enjoyable and delectable as I do. Follow the recipes step by step or add in your own hocus-pocus. Whether you're a seasoned ghost or a culinary hobgoblin in training, join me on this nightmare as we summon spicy spirits and have a ghastly good time. Grab your cauldron, sharpen your wooden stakes, and let's make your kitchen creepy.

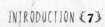

Tools & Equipment

Here are the ghostly kitchen tools and equipment that you'll need to make these creepy-licious recipes.

* 8 × 8-inch (20 × 20 cm) baking dish or pan

* 9 × 13-inch (23 × 33 cm) cake pan

* 9 × 13-inch (23 × 33 cm) casserole dish

* 12-cup muffin pan

* 24-cup mini muffin pan

* Aluminum foil

* Apple corer

* Baking sheets, half and quarter sizes

* Basting bulb

* Bento food picks, eye-style

* Candy thermometer

* Cocktail shaker

* Cookie cutters: gingerbread man, large circle, mini bat, mini crescent, mini ghost, mini heart, and mini pumpkin

* Cookie scoops, size 40

* Craft sticks

* Cupcake liners

* Deviled egg platter

* Dutch oven with lid

* Flour sifter

* Food-grade disposable gloves

* Food processor with blade attachment

* Ice cream scoop

* Icing bag

* Immersion blender

* Kitchen shears

* Krampus or goat head flat silhouette, about 2" (5 cm) in diameter

* Large skillet or frying pan

* Liquid measuring cup

* Mandoline slicer

* Meat mallet

* Meat thermometer

* Non-slip silicone baking mat

* Offset spatula

* Paper lollipop sticks

* Parchment paper

* Pastry brush

* Piping tips

* Plastic wrap

* Potato masher

* Roasting pan

* Roomy sealable containers

* Rubber spatula

* Serving platter or board

* Silicone ice pop mold with reusable sticks

* Slow cooker or pressure cooker with slow cooker setting

* Soup pot, 4 quart (3.8 L)

* Stand mixer with dough, whisk, and paddle attachments or handheld mixer

* Swizzle sticks

* Toothpicks

* Vegetable peeler

* Wax paper

* Whisk

* Wire cooling rack

* Wooden skewers

Shuddersome Starters & Drinks for Darklings

Sink your fangs into some tantalizingly terror-ific appetizers, guaranteed to set the mood for a hauntingly delightful feast. Your friends, family, and guests will be transfixed by tormentingly tasty morsels, from creepy clown dips to bone-chilling finger foods and shady soup. But the terror won't end there! As the moon rises and the night deepens, indulge in the mixology of otherworldly elixirs, sure to quench the most insatiable vampire's thirst. These sublime sips will keep anyone mystically mesmerized.

Apple Wassail Mimosas

MAKES 6 TO 8 MIMOSAS

Apple Wassail is a centuries-old nighttime ceremony occurring in some of southern England's cider apple orchards. Its roots lie in pagan rituals, from awakening apple trees from their winter slumber to offering blessings for the coming growing season. Combine apple cider and prosecco to create a seasonal mimosa rimmed with honey and cinnamon sugar. Use sparkling white grape juice to make this a nonalcoholic delight for everyone and enjoy this seasonal take on a traditional brunch classic.

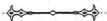

SPECIAL EQUIPMENT NEEDED

Mini ghost cookie cutter, 6 to 8 champagne flutes (or any tall glasses)

INGREDIENTS

¼ cup (50 g) granulated sugar

2 teaspoons ground cinnamon

2 tablespoons honey

1 apple

1 cup (240 ml) brandy

8 cups (2 L) apple cider

1 bottle (750 ml) chilled prosecco

1. In a small bowl, combine the sugar and cinnamon.

2. Pour the honey into a separate small bowl.

3. With a sharp knife, cut ⅛-inch-thick (3 mm) vertical slices from the side of the apple. Using the mini ghost cookie cutter, stamp out ghosts for garnish. Make a ¼-inch (6 mm) slice in the bottom of each ghost for easy placement on the rims of the champagne flutes.

4. Dip the rims of the champagne flutes into the honey, then dip them into the cinnamon-sugar mixture. Delicately tap off any excess.

5. Pour 1 teaspoon of brandy into each flute. Fill one-third to one-half of the flute with apple cider.

6. Slowly pour the chilled prosecco over the apple cider until the flutes are nearly full. Pour gently to preserve the bubbles. Gently stir the mimosas.

7. Place the ghost apple garnish on the rims of the flutes.

8. Serve immediately while the drink is still bubbly and cold.

HEED: The ratio of prosecco to apple cider can be adjusted based on personal preference. Some people prefer equal parts of both, while others like more prosecco for more bubbles. Experiment and find the balance that suits your taste.

Wednesday's Wicked Figgy Treats

MAKES ABOUT 24 TREATS

As the nursery rhyme goes, "Wednesday's child is full of woe." But with Wednesday's Wicked Figgy Treats, you're more likely to be full of "Whoa!" In this creation, sweetness meets tang in the kookiest of contrasts. Rich, purple fig jam dances with sharp, creamy white goat cheese, all atop a crispy crostini—much like the spellbinding, arm-flailing dance a certain Nevermore Academy student does at the Rave'N. These darkly delightful appetizers are a surprising addition to any gathering, offering a marvelously morose balance of flavors and textures.

INGREDIENTS

1 small baguette or Italian bread loaf (about 11 inches, or 28 cm, long)

3 tablespoons extra-virgin olive oil

6 ounces (170 g) goat cheese

8½ ounces (240 g) fig spread

⅓ cup (40 g) slivered almonds

1 tablespoon fresh thyme leaves

Fresh thyme sprigs, for garnish

DID YOU KNOW?

Charles Addams, born in 1912, was an American cartoonist renowned for creating The Addams Family. Debuting in *The New Yorker* in 1938, his macabre and darkly humorous cartoons introduced a quirky, wealthy family with a penchant for things frightening and bizarre.

1. Preheat the oven to 375°F (190°C, or gas mark 5).

2. Slice the baguette or Italian bread into ½-inch-thick (12 mm) slices. Cut them on a slight diagonal for a larger surface area, if desired. Place the bread slices on a baking sheet and brush one side of each slice with olive oil.

3. Put the baking sheet in the oven and toast the bread slices for 5 to 7 minutes, until they turn golden brown and crispy. Keep a close eye on them to avoid burning.

4. Remove the bread slices from the oven and let them cool for 2 to 3 minutes on a wire rack.

5. Spread 1 to 2 teaspoons of goat cheese on each of the bread slices.

6. Spoon a generous dollop of fig spread onto each goat cheese–covered bread slice. (Adjust the amounts of cheese and fig spread to your liking.)

7. Sprinkle each slice with almond and thyme leaves. Top with a small sprig of thyme.

8. Arrange the prepared crostini on a serving platter and serve immediately.

HEED: These are best when they're freshly made, so your guests can enjoy the crispy texture.

Double Double Toil and Trouble Feta Beet Dip in a Bread Cauldron

MAKES 8 TO 10 SERVINGS

Double, double, toil and trouble, fire burn and a concoction of feta and beets shall bubble, up and over a cauldron of sourdough. No filet of fenny snakes, eye of newt, nor toes of frog to be found here, just the earthy flavors of briny feta and sweet beets entwining to create a tangy and savory potion sure to please the palate. This sorcery-inspired dip is both visually captivating and delicious, making it a must-have treat for an enchanted festive gathering.

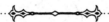

SPECIAL EQUIPMENT NEEDED

Food processor with a blade attachment

INGREDIENTS

1 sourdough boule or round bread loaf of choice (14 ounces, or 397 g)

2 or 3 medium beets, scrubbed clean, or 1 package (8 ounces, or 225 g) ready-to-eat beets

8 ounces (225 g) feta cheese, crumbled and at room temperature

6 ounces (170 g) cream cheese

2 tablespoons extra-virgin olive oil

1 or 2 cloves garlic, minced

2 teaspoons lemon juice

¼ teaspoon salt

¼ teaspoon red pepper flakes

1 bag (9 ounces, or 255 g) blue corn tortilla chips

1 bag (8.5 ounces, or 240 g) crunchy cheese-flavored snacks (such as Cheetos)

1 medium cucumber, cut into spears

1. To make the bread cauldron: Carefully cut off the top of the bread loaf and set it aside. Hollow out the inside, removing excess bread to create a bowl-like interior shape. Make sure to leave enough bread on the sides and bottom to maintain structural integrity. Cut the bread top and inside bread pieces into bite-size pieces and set them aside.

2. Preheat the oven to 400°F (205°C, or gas mark 6). If using raw beets, trim off their tops and bottoms and individually wrap them tightly in foil. Place the wrapped beets on a baking sheet in case any juice leaks out. Roast for 35 minutes to 1 hour, until they can be easily pierced with a fork. Once they are cool enough to touch, unfold from foil and rub skin off using a paper towel.

3. Whether using ready-to-eat beets or roasted beets, next chop beets into small chunks. Place the feta cheese, cream cheese, olive oil, beets, minced garlic, lemon juice, salt, and pepper flakes in a food processor with a blade attachment. Process ingredients until smooth and creamy, scraping down the sides as needed. The mixture should be a beautiful creamy pink-to-purple color and have a whipped consistency. Taste and adjust the seasonings.

4. Place the cauldron on a serving platter and fill with dip. Arrange remaining bread, blue corn tortilla chips, crunchy cheese snacks, and cucumbers around the cauldron to look like kindling and fire.

Sausage Biscuit Brains

MAKES ABOUT 3 DOZEN BRAINS

Brains in jars, brains as main characters, disembodied brains . . . How many movies have you seen where brains take center stage? *Man with the Screaming Brain* (2005), *Mars Attacks!* (1996), *The Brain* (1988), *The Man with Two Brains* (1983), *Young Frankenstein* (1974), and *Fiend Without a Face* (1958) are just a sampling. These savory and chewy Sausage Biscuit Brains may not be the star of the show, but they steal the spotlight as a substantial appetizer or hors d'oeuvres.

SPECIAL EQUIPMENT NEEDED
Food processor, food-grade disposable gloves

INGREDIENTS
2 cups (250 g) all-purpose flour

1½ tablespoons baking powder

½ teaspoon salt

3 tablespoons butter, cold and sliced

1 pound (454 g) ground sausage, uncooked

4 cups (460 g) shredded sharp Cheddar cheese

1 teaspoon hot sauce, or to taste

1. Preheat the oven to 400°F (205°C, or gas mark 6). Line two half baking sheets with parchment paper or non-slip silicone baking mats.

2. Place the flour, baking powder, salt, and butter into a food processor. Pulse until mixture is the consistency of coarse sand.

3. In a separate large bowl, combine the flour mixture, sausage, cheese, and hot sauce. Gloved hands work best.

4. Roll mixture into 1-inch (2.5 cm) balls. Using a butter knife, score each ball down the middle. Slightly separate the sides to create the 2 hemispheres of the brain.

5. Arrange the balls on the prepared baking sheets.

6. Bake for 15 to 20 minutes, until browned. The brains should have an internal temperature of 160°F (71°C) when done.

7. The brains will puff up while baking and may need to be scored again once out of the oven.

8. These are best served warm.

HEED: These are great for freezing! While they are on the baking sheets, place uncooked brains in a freezer for 2 to 4 hours. Once solid, place frozen brains in a freezer bag. They can be kept for 2 to 3 months. They may also be frozen after baking.

Cauliflower Coulrophobia Dip Tray

MAKES 10 SERVINGS

To celebrate Halloween, a truly terrifying culinary creation is in order—a simple crudité and dip tray, arranged just so, to resemble a clown of your nightmares.

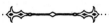

INGREDIENTS

DIP

½ cup (120 ml) mayonnaise

½ cup (120 ml) plain Greek yogurt

2 tablespoons minced red onion

1½ teaspoons curry powder

½ teaspoon lemon juice

¼ teaspoon salt

Zest of 1 lemon

CLOWN CRUDITÉ

1 large cauliflower head, leaves removed

1 pint (400 g) cherry tomatoes

1 red pepper, cored and seeded

2 pita breads, sliced into wedges

4 carrots, peeled and cut into 16 sticks

1 celery stalk, cut into 16 sticks

4 garlic scapes

1 seedless cucumber, thinly sliced

1. To make the dip: In a small bowl, stir together the mayonnaise, yogurt, onion, curry powder, lemon juice, salt, and lemon zest. Cover and chill overnight. Fill a small serving bowl with dip.

2. To create the clown crudité: Place the cauliflower head on a cutting board, stem side down. Using a sharp knife, make one big vertical cut through one side of the head. Set the slice aside to be the clown's forehead. Place the remaining cauliflower stem side up, and cut along the core to separate florets. Try to keep large florets together and stems intact. Organize florets by size.

3. On a large platter or board, place the small bowl of dip on the lower part of the platter, where the clown's mouth will be. Arrange the clown face: Use the large cauliflower slice for the forehead. Leaving space empty for the eye sockets, add florets to the sides for temples and a long floret (stem side up) in between for the nasal bone/nose. Continue to work down the face with florets for cheeks and jaw. Fill in around the dip bowl for the upper lip area and chin. Fill any empty areas with smaller florets. Add dimension under florets with cauliflower stem slices. Use toothpicks to hold florets in place where needed.

4. Put 5 or 6 cherry tomatoes into each eye socket.

5. Cut the red pepper into 4 quarters, from top to bottom. Slash snaggle-tooth details into each. Place around the dip bowl for fangs.

6. Use the pita bread to create a spiky crown at the top of the head. Bunch carrot and celery sticks together to form hair. Cut and wind the garlic scapes into circles, securing with toothpicks and add around the clown face to look like a clown collar. Fill empty spaces with cucumber slices and cherry tomatoes.

Sinister Spiders

MAKES 12 DEVILED EGGS

Once upon a midnight dreary, a spider perched on an egg so eerie. Its legs crossed the tasty treat, as the spider savored its devilish feat. But as it took another bite, a searing pain filled it with fright. The egg exacted its revenge, leaving the spider a fiery end.

SPECIAL EQUIPMENT NEEDED

Food-grade disposable gloves, deviled egg platter or serving platter

INGREDIENTS

2 tablespoons white vinegar

8 to 10 drops super black gel food coloring

6 hard-boiled eggs, shells on and cooled

¼ cup (60 ml) mayonnaise

1 teaspoon yellow mustard

¼ teaspoon dill

Dash salt and ground black pepper

2 tablespoons finely chopped or minced sweet pickles

2 teaspoons sweet pickle juice

1 can (6 ounces, or 170 g) pitted black olives, extra large

¼ teaspoon paprika (optional)

1. Mix 2 cups (480 ml) of water with the vinegar, and black gel food coloring in a large bowl. Using a spoon or countertop, tap each egg to create cracks all over shell. Place the eggs in the bowl of dye mixture. Let soak for 1 to 2 hours in the refrigerator. (If bowl is shallow, soak eggs for 30 minutes and then turn to ensure evenness of dye exposure.)

2. Now is the time to wear food-grade disposable gloves, because handling the dyed egg shells will stain your hands and fingernails. Remove eggs from dye mixture and pat dry with a paper towel. Gently peel eggs, being careful not to rip egg whites. Cut hard-boiled eggs in half lengthwise. Remove yolks and place in a medium bowl. Place egg whites on a platter or egg plate.

3. Mash the yolks with a fork until they resemble a sandy texture. Add the mayonnaise, mustard, dill, salt, and pepper and stir until well combined and smooth. (Little salt is added due to the saltiness of the black olives that will be placed on top.) Mix in pickles and pickle juice until combined. Cover and refrigerate for 30 minutes for mixture to slightly firm up.

4. Slice 6 olives lengthwise; this will give you 12 spider bodies. Slice another 10–12 olives lengthwise. Then thinly slice each half 5–6 times crosswise. These are the spiders' legs. The legs can be delicate and break in two, so slice more legs than you think you need.

5. Remove egg yolk mixture from the refrigerator. To keep it simple, spoon about 1 to 2 teaspoons of yolk mixture into each egg half. To level up, place yolk mixture in a piping bag fitted with a large open tip or a plastic sandwich bag with a bottom corner cut off. Pipe yolk mixture into the cavity of each egg white.

6. On each egg half, place one spider body surrounded by 8 legs. Sprinkle with paprika if desired and place on serving platter.

The Great Pumpkin Curry Soup

MAKES ABOUT 6 SERVINGS

Did part of this soup rise from the pumpkin patch on Halloween night to give presents to good children? ABSOLUTELY! That's what makes it taste so good. It's also delicious because the sweet, earthy flavor of pumpkin combines with the rich, aromatic zest of curry to create a comforting dish you'll have no problem missing out on or trick-or-treating for.

SPECIAL EQUIPMENT NEEDED

Dutch oven or soup pot, immersion blender

INGREDIENTS

2 tablespoons unsalted butter

½ pound (227 g) white mushrooms, sliced

1 small yellow onion, diced

2 tablespoons all-purpose flour

1 teaspoon to 1 tablespoon curry powder, depending on your preferred spice level

3 cups (720 ml) chicken or vegetable broth

1 can (15 ounces, or 425 g) pumpkin purée

1½ cups (360 ml) half-and-half, or unsweetened milk of choice

1 tablespoon honey

¼ teaspoon ground nutmeg

¼ teaspoon dried thyme

Salt and ground black pepper, to taste

Finely chopped fresh chives for garnish (optional)

1. In a Dutch oven or soup pot over medium heat, melt the butter. Add the mushrooms and onion and cook, stirring occasionally, until soft, about 5 minutes.

2. Stir in the flour and curry powder until completely blended. Cook for 1 minute.

3. Gradually add the broth. Scrape any seasonings off the bottom of the pot. Bring to a boil over high heat and cook for 2 minutes, or until thickened.

4. Add the pumpkin, half-and-half, honey, nutmeg, and thyme and stir until completely combined. Reduce the heat to medium for 5 to 10 minutes, until the soup is heated through. Do not let it boil.

5. Purée with an immersion blender, then season with salt and pepper.

6. Serve hot. Garnish with chopped chives if desired.

DID YOU KNOW?

The Greatest Pumpkin ever documented by Guinness World Records was 2,749 pounds (1,247 kg) and grown in Minnesota.

Shark Bite Sipper

MAKES 4 SIPPERS

In the ocean's vast expanse resides a creature that haunts the nightmares of sailors, swimmers, and moviegoers alike: the shark. With teeth as sharp as daggers, these ancient predators prowl the depths with a sinister elegance. The Shark Bite Sipper brings the ocean's most formidable dweller into your glass with vivid blue curaçao, vodka, lemon-lime soda, and a toy shark filled with vengeance and grenadine. When emptied of its red contents, this solitary shark unleashes a terror that mirrors the fate of its next meal. Sip this slowly, and as you do, contemplate the fear and fascination of what waits beneath the surface of the ocean.

SPECIAL EQUIPMENT NEEDED

Cocktail shaker, 4 wide-mouth glasses, 4 hollow shark toys, 4 swizzle sticks

INGREDIENTS

¼ cup (60 ml) blue curaçao

½ cup (120 ml) vodka

4 cups (960 ml) ice cubes

2 cups (480 ml) lemon-lime soda

8 to 12 tablespoons grenadine syrup

DID YOU KNOW?

Although no confirmed instances of Sharknados exist, tornadoes and waterspouts can lift aquatic animals such as fish and alligators and potentially deposit them inland.

1. Fill the cocktail shaker with the blue curaçao and vodka. Gently shake the mixture.

2. Evenly pour the mixture into 4 glasses. Fill the glasses with ice cubes and slowly add the lemon-lime soda, filling about three-fourths full, being careful not to disturb the blue vodka mixture.

3. Pour the grenadine syrup into the shark toys and carefully place one in each glass, mouth pointed up. If you do not have a shark, add 2 or 3 dashes of grenadine syrup to the drink top.

4. Add the swizzle sticks and serve with instructions to pour out the shark's contents, thus instigating a shark attack in a glass.

HEED: Ingredient proportions can be adjusted based on personal taste preferences. To make a nonalcoholic version, serve as a Shirley Temple, with grenadine syrup and lemon-lime soda. Pour the lemon-lime soda over ice, filling the glass about three-fourths full. Add the grenadine syrup and a cherry. The grenadine will sink to the bottom of the glass and create a layered look. Add a slice of orange or a twist of lemon as an additional garnish for added flavor and aesthetic.

Mask of the Red Death Ice Scream Float

MAKES 4 FLOATS

In a chilling twist, the strange and most offensive guest of Prince Prospero's party in Poe's "The Masque of the Red Death" takes on the frosty form of an ice cream float. The gaudy embodiment of Red Death is neither a knight nor lady but layers of crimson-red tropical punch soda, vanilla ice cream, pink frothy foam, and fluffy whipped cream topped with black sprinkles and gummy death-heads. So sweet and delicious, you might not remember this partier is an impostor.

SPECIAL EQUIPMENT NEEDED

4 tall glasses, 4 straws

INGREDIENTS

1 box (1.7 ounces, or 45 g) watermelon and cherry crunchy candy (such as Nerds)

2 tablespoons vanilla frosting

1 tub (1.5 quarts, or 1.4 L) vanilla ice cream

¾ cup (180 ml) light or spiced rum (1½ ounces, or 45 ml, in each glass) (optional)

6½ cups (1.5 L) fruit punch–flavored or red-colored soda

Whipped cream

12 separated pieces cherry or red pull-apart licorice, cut into fourths

12 skull gummies (3 skewered vertically on a toothpick for 4 total toothpicks)

Black sanding sugar, for topping

1. Empty the crunchy candy into a small shallow bowl.

2. Spread the frosting along the rims of 4 tall glasses, then dip the frosted rims into the crunchy candy. Twist the glasses to make sure the entire rims are covered in candy.

3. Scoop ice cream into each glass. You can use one or more scoops, depending on how creamy and rich you want your float to be and the size of your glass.

4. Slowly add the rum, if using, then pour the soda over the ice cream until the glass is about three-fourths full. Pour slowly to prevent excessive foaming and keep the crunchy candy from being disturbed.

5. Add the whipped cream, licorice, and toothpicks of skulls. Sprinkle sanding sugar on top and add a straw.

HEED: To make this drink nonalcoholic, simply remove the rum and add additional fruit punch soda. It remains just as delicious!

DID YOU KNOW?

"The Masque of the Red Death" by Edgar Allan Poe is a short story first published in *Graham's Magazine* in May 1842. Poe pioneered the modern short story with his tales of mystery and horror, influencing generations of writers.

Whipped Pumpkin Spice Latte

MAKES 2 LATTES

Life is gourd when it's Pumpkin Spice Latte season! Combining the warm, cozy flavors of fall with trendy and frothy coffee, this is a pumpkin patch party in your mouth. Maple syrup, pumpkin purée, and milk make a delicious base for a foamy crown on a strong whipped coffee. It's a beautiful multilayered drink—just make sure to stir before drinking!

SPECIAL EQUIPMENT NEEDED

Stand mixer with whisk attachment or handheld mixer, small saucepan

INGREDIENTS

1 tablespoon instant coffee

½ teaspoon pumpkin spice mix, plus more for topping

2 tablespoons granulated sugar

3 tablespoons hot water

1 cup (240 ml) milk of choice

3 tablespoons pumpkin purée

2 tablespoons maple syrup

1 teaspoon vanilla extract

DID YOU KNOW?

The earliest-known reference to pumpkin spice can be traced back to a British recipe from 1675. The term referred to a combination of spices used in cooking, including pepper, cloves, nutmeg, and cinnamon. The first modern Pumpkin Spice Latte was created at Starbucks' Seattle headquarters in 2003.

1. In the bowl of a stand mixer with a whisk attachment, or a medium bowl with a handheld mixer, combine the instant coffee, pumpkin spice mix, sugar, and hot water. Whisk on high for 2 to 4 minutes. The mixture will turn from a dark brown liquid to a thick, golden caramel froth.

2. Add the milk, pumpkin purée, and maple syrup to a small saucepan over medium heat and whisk until well combined. Heat through until just about to simmer. Do not let the mixture boil. Take off the heat and whisk in the vanilla.

3. Fill each serving glass or mug two-thirds full with maple pumpkin milk, leaving room for the whipped coffee.

4. Spoon the whipped coffee mixture on top of the milk. Sprinkle with additional pumpkin spice mix. The resulting whipped coffee drink will be 2 layers: maple pumpkin milk on the bottom and rich, frothy coffee on top.

5. Serve with a spoon or a straw to mix the layers together. Stir the whipped coffee into the milk before drinking.

HEED: If you prefer a cold beverage, follow directions for whipped coffee and then only heat the milk enough to dissolve the pumpkin and maple syrup. Pour the maple pumpkin milk over ice and then add the whipped coffee.

Haunted Hot Hot Chocolate

MAKES 3 OR 4 SERVINGS

Inspired by Mexican hot chocolate, this sweet combination of delightfully dark cocoa powder, brown sugar, and autumnal seasonings creates a velvety chocolate drink. For a tantalizing twist, pinches of chili powder and cayenne pepper add bold and fiery kicks. Savor this creation as a nonalcoholic treat, perfect for cozy evenings as nights grow longer and the temperature grows colder. Alternatively, embark on a flavor adventure by pairing it with tequila blanco for a tasty blend of rich chocolate and earthy agave notes.

INGREDIENTS

4 cups (960 ml) milk of choice

⅓ cup (57 g) brown sugar

¼ cup (30 g) unsweetened cocoa powder

¾ teaspoon ground cinnamon

¼ teaspoon salt

Dash chili powder

Dash cayenne pepper

2 teaspoons vanilla extract

½ cup (120 ml) tequila blanco (optional)

Whipped cream, for topping

Chocolate shavings, for topping

Sugar strand sprinkles, for topping

1. In a medium saucepan over medium-low heat, combine the milk, brown sugar, cocoa powder, cinnamon, salt, chili powder, and cayenne pepper. Whisk frequently until warm to hot, but not boiling.

2. Remove from the heat and stir in the vanilla and tequila, if using.

3. Serve in mugs topped with whipped cream and sprinkled with chocolate shavings and sugar strand sprinkles.

DID YOU KNOW?

Mexican hot chocolate is deeply rooted in Mexican culture and culinary traditions, with a history dating back to ancient Mayan and Aztec civilizations. It is made with solid chocolate in the form of tablets or disks, which are made from ground roasted cocoa beans mixed with sugar and flavored with spices such as cinnamon. The hot chocolate has a thick and slightly grainy texture due to the use of solid chocolate.

Boogeyman Bourbon Bramble

MAKES 4 BRAMBLES

Things might get spooky when you sip a Boogeyman Bourbon Bramble. The murky depths of this bittersweet cocktail pay homage to the ominous Boogeyman, a nightmarish creature who lurks in the shadows and under your bed. An interesting riff on a traditional Blackberry Bramble, this version blends bourbon's smoky notes with elderflower liqueur's floral essence, crème de cassis' dark sweetness, and lemon's acidic twinge. Don't be afraid to serve this delicious demonic drink . . . just make sure all of your lights are on.

SPECIAL EQUIPMENT NEEDED

Cocktail shaker, 4 coupe cocktail glasses

INGREDIENTS

¼ cup (60 ml) bourbon

2 tablespoons elderflower liqueur

2 tablespoons crème de cassis liqueur

2 tablespoons lemon juice (freshly squeezed if possible) or to taste

2 or 3 dashes aromatic bitters, or to taste

1 to 2 cups (240 to 470 ml) ice cubes

1 lemon, for garnish

8 vampire teeth gummies (2 skewered on a toothpick for 4 total toothpicks), for garnish

1. In a cocktail shaker, combine the bourbon, elderflower liqueur, crème de cassis, lemon juice, and aromatic bitters. (Adjust the amount of lemon juice and bitters based on your preferred tastes.)

2. Add the ice cubes to the shaker and shake the mixture vigorously for 10 to 15 seconds. Along with mixing, this will chill the ingredients and properly dilute the cocktail.

3. Using a cocktail strainer, pour the shaken mixture into 4 coupe cocktail glasses. This will strain out any ice chips.

4. To make the garnish: Wash the lemon, cut off the ends, and use a knife or peeler to remove the thin layer of peel, avoiding pith. Trim to size, about ½-inch to 2 inches (1 to 5 cm). Fold peel in half and ease on to middle of toothpick. Sandwich two gummy vampire teeth between lemon peel to make it creepy.

5. Add garnishes to the glasses, serve, and enjoy! Sip it slowly to savor the flavors and aromas.

DID YOU KNOW?

Baba Roga, a character from Southern Slavic folklore, is a fearsome boogeyman of a grandma who frightens children into good behavior. She's big and stocky, has a horn growing from the middle of her forehead, and lives in a mystical dark cave. Although she is an antagonist in a number of wicked folktales, she is not purely evil. Baba Roga also visits sleeping children to make sure they have pleasant dreams. If they wake up, she scares them back to sleep. Her sister is Baba Yaga.

Bewitching Bites & Shadowy Sides

Cast a spell on your taste buds with this collection of treacherous snacks and sides! Designed to tame peckish pumpkin-carvers and half-starved trick-or-treaters, tidbits such as skeletal pretzels and extraterrestrial dates are quick to prepare. They can help the greediest of ghosts power through graveyard gatherings and fright fests. Much like iconic duos such as Morticia and Gomez or Shrek and Fiona, side dishes of darling dinner rolls and supernatural macaroni and cheese will complement and complete any main course. Beware, for these nefarious nibbles may possess some kind of cooked charm that lures even cautious souls to the table.

Dinner Roll Pumpkins

MAKES 20 PUMPKINS

Behold one of the cutest manifestations of the season—a bread roll transformed into an adorable and tasty pumpkin.

SPECIAL EQUIPMENT NEEDED

Stand mixer with paddle attachment and dough hook, pastry brush

INGREDIENTS

2¼ teaspoons instant or rapid-rise yeast

½ cup (120 ml) warm water

½ cup (100 g) packed brown sugar

1 cup (250 g) pumpkin purée

½ cup (120 ml) warm milk of choice

½ cup (1 stick or 115 g) unsalted butter, melted and cooled

1 teaspoon pumpkin pie spice

2 teaspoons salt

4 cups (500 g) all-purpose flour, divided

Cooking oil spray

1 egg, beaten, for egg wash

1 teaspoon heavy cream, for egg wash

10 pretzel sticks, broken in half

HEED: For an alternative way to make pumpkins, see page 150.

1. In a stand mixer with a paddle attachment, combine the yeast, warm water, and brown sugar. Then stir in the pumpkin, milk, melted butter, pumpkin pie spice, salt, and 3 cups (375 g) of the flour. Scrape down sides as needed. Add remaining 1 cup (125 g) flour and combine until a sticky dough forms. Switch stand mixer attachment to dough hook. Knead for 5 to 7 minutes, until dough is smooth and elastic and clings to hook.

2. Place dough in a greased bowl and cover it with a clean kitchen towel. Let the dough rise in a warm place, such as your oven. (Preheat oven to 200°F, or 90°C, or gas mark 1 for 1 to 2 minutes, then turn it off. Place the covered bowl of dough inside the oven.) Let rise for 1 to 2 hours, until doubled in size.

3. Line a baking sheet with parchment paper. Lightly grease the parchment paper with cooking oil spray.

4. Carefully punch down the dough with your hands. Cut the dough into 4 equal pieces, then cut each piece into 5 pieces to make 20 dough pieces. Shape each portion into a small ball.

5. Using kitchen shears or scissors, make 6 to 8 vertical snips or cuts around the edges of each roll, about ½-inch (13 mm), into the center of the dough. Dough sections will resemble the sections of a pumpkin. Place rolls on a baking sheet, leaving at least 1 inch (2.5 cm) of space between them. Cover with a kitchen towel and let rise for 30 minutes.

6. Preheat the oven to 375°F (190°C, or gas mark 5).

7. In a small bowl, whisk together the egg and heavy cream to make the egg wash. Using a pastry brush, brush the pumpkins with egg wash. Bake for 15 to 20 minutes, until golden brown.

8. Remove the rolls from oven. After rolls cool for 3 to 5 minutes, insert a half pretzel stick into the top of each roll to resemble a pumpkin stem. Serve warm.

Whisper & Scream Mac & Cheese

MAKES 10 TO 12 SERVINGS

A devilish blend of cheeses and a bewitching mix of spices come together to beguile your taste buds and make you shriek with delight. Beware, this dish is not for the faint of heart nor faint of appetite—prepare to be enchanted by its savory charms!

INGREDIENTS

Cooking oil spray

8 ounces (198 g) macaroni (elbow) pasta

1 tablespoon salt, for pasta water

¼ cup (57 g) cream cheese

1 cup (240 ml) milk of choice

½ teaspoon smoked paprika

1 teaspoon garlic powder

½ teaspoon onion powder

½ teaspoon mustard powder

¼ teaspoon ground black pepper

⅛ teaspoon ground nutmeg

1 cup (115 g) shredded Colby Jack cheese

½ cup (58 g) shredded mozzarella cheese

1 cup (115 g) shredded Edam cheese

2 cups (230 g) shredded Cheddar cheese, divided

2 eggs

1 cup (76 g) cheese snack crackers (such as Cheez-It), crushed into crumbs

1. Preheat the oven to 350°F (175°C, or gas mark 5). Grease a 9 × 13-inch (23 × 33 cm) casserole dish with cooking oil spray.

2. Cook the pasta in boiling salted water according to package directions. Cook al dente because the pasta will continue to cook while baking. Drain pasta, reserving 1 cup (240 ml) of the pasta cooking water.

3. Return the pasta to the pot. Add the cream cheese and reserved pasta water. Stir until cream cheese is melted.

4. In a large bowl, whisk together the milk and cooled pasta water. Add the smoked paprika, garlic powder, onion powder, mustard powder, pepper, and nutmeg. Add the Colby Jack, mozzarella, Edam, and 1 cup (115 g) of the Cheddar. Use a spoon or spatula to combine everything, then stir in the cooked pasta and eggs until well incorporated.

5. Spoon the pasta and cheese mixture into the prepared casserole dish. Sprinkle the top with the remaining 1 cup (115 g) Cheddar and the cheese snack cracker crumbs.

6. Bake uncovered for 30 minutes, or until the cheese has melted and browned. Let cool for about 10 minutes before serving.

HEED: Unbaked macaroni and cheese can be frozen for up to 3 months.

Invasion of the Brussels Sprouts

MAKES 4 SERVINGS

Were you around in the 1990s when brussels sprouts, once the stuff of nightmares, transformed into a better tasting trendy side dish? Thanks to a Dutch scientist/wizard and traditional plant breeding, brussels sprouts left their mushy, bitter past behind and emerged as a mellow, almost nutty-flavored vegetable that is now enjoyed by most . . . . Or did some kind of unknown entity from outer space crash-land near a small town and begin to take over the minds and palates of innocent citizens just looking to get their two to three cups of vegetables a day? You be the judge, but in the meantime, try these slightly sweet and savory sprouts that bring both heat and tang.

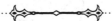

INGREDIENTS

2 tablespoons olive oil, divided

2 tablespoons honey

2 tablespoons hot chili sauce (such as Sriracha), or to taste

1 tablespoon soy sauce or tamari

1 pound (454 g) brussels sprouts, trimmed and halved

1. In a small bowl, combine 1 tablespoon of the olive oil, honey, hot chili sauce, and soy sauce. Whisk until well combined.

2. In a large skillet over medium heat, heat the remaining 1 tablespoon olive oil. Add the brussels sprouts, cut sides down and cook for 8 to 12 minutes, periodically shaking the pan to prevent sticking. Flip several sprouts to check if bottoms are beautifully caramelized; if not, continue cooking for 2 to 3 more minutes and check again. Once caramelization is achieved, flip all the sprouts and cook for another 3 to 5 minutes, shaking the pan periodically.

3. Reduce the heat to medium-low. Drizzle the sauce over the sprouts and gently toss to evenly coat. Cook for an additional 1 to 3 minutes to heat through.

4. Remove from the heat and serve.

DID YOU KNOW?

The reason some people love brussels sprouts while others dislike them is a gene called TAS2R38. This gene controls our ability to taste the bitter compound PTC, which is found in sprouts. Different variations of TAS2R38 can influence our perception of bitterness, explaining why preferences for sprouts vary among individuals and families.

All Souls' Potatoes

MAKES 4 SERVINGS

If you've ever carved a pumpkin, you can carve a potato. Start simple with a sharp paring knife; cut pyramids for eyes and noses and wedges for smiles. Dig into the potato with a vegetable peeler's potato eyer to make hollow eyes and gaping, wailing mouths. (A potato eyer is a scoop or nub at the tip, or a cutout on the side, of a vegetable peeler used to remove potato eyes.)

SPECIAL EQUIPMENT NEEDED

Dutch oven with lid or deep oven-proof skillet or soup pot

INGREDIENTS

2 tablespoons lemon juice or white vinegar

24 ounces (680 g) baby medley potatoes

⅓ cup (80 ml) extra-virgin olive oil

1 large onion, diced

3 cloves garlic, minced

6 plum tomatoes or 1 can (15 ounces, or 411 g) whole peeled tomatoes, diced

½ teaspoon salt

¼ teaspoon pepper

2 or 3 sprigs flat-leaf parsley, minced (optional)

1. In a large bowl, combine 1 quart (1 L) of water with the lemon juice. This will hold your potatoes once they are carved.

2. Use your imagination and knife skills to carefully carve traditional pumpkin faces, stone statue faces, ghost visages, and whatever horrid heads you can imagine. These are shrunken heads, so perfection is not the goal. As you finish each head, place in the bowl of lemon water.

3. In a Dutch oven over medium-high heat, heat the olive oil. Add the onion and cook, stirring occasionally, the onion for 5 minutes, or until it starts to brown. Add the garlic and cook for 30 seconds, or until aromatic.

4. Add tomatoes, salt, and pepper to the pan and stir to combine. Cook on low for 5 minutes.

5. Drain the potato heads and pat dry.

6. Preheat the oven to 350°F (175°C, or gas mark 4).

7. Add the potato heads to the Dutch oven, stirring to make sure they are completely covered in the sauce. Simmer on low for 10 minutes, stirring occasionally. Taste and adjust seasoning if necessary.

8. Cover the pan with the lid and place in the oven. Cook for 40 minutes to 1 hour, until potato heads can easily be pierced with a fork.

9. Garnish with minced parsley, if using, and serve.

Corn-iverous Ribs

MAKES 32 CORN RIBS

In the peculiar realm of culinary curiosities, a most confounding dish emerged from trending Tik Tok recipes—a creation of savory ribs, fashioned not from the usual fare, but from corn! These Corn-iverous Ribs are chewy and delicious, wrapped in the monstrous flavors of chili, garlic, and paprika. You will be both perplexed and tantalized, left to ponder these whimsical wonders as riddles once wrapped in a husk.

SPECIAL EQUIPMENT NEEDED

Soup pot

INGREDIENTS

4 ears corn, shucked and cleaned

¼ cup (55 g) unsalted butter, melted

1 teaspoon chili powder

1 teaspoon garlic powder

1 teaspoon paprika

½ teaspoon onion powder

½ teaspoon salt

⅛ teaspoon ground black pepper

Spicy Creepy Crema (see page 82), or BBQ sauce of choice, for serving

1. Fill a large soup pot halfway full of water and bring it to a boil over high heat. Place corn in boiling water and let boil for 10 minutes. Drain and cool for 5 to 10 minutes, until safe to touch.

2. Preheat the oven to 425°F (220°C, or gas mark 7). Line a half baking sheet with parchment paper.

3. Cut each ear of corn into 8 slices. With a very sharp knife, trim off both ends. Cut each ear in half, and then cut each half into quarters. Repeat with remaining corn.

4. In a large bowl, stir together the melted butter, chili powder, garlic powder, paprika, onion powder, salt, and pepper.

5. Add the corn ribs to the bowl and mix thoroughly. Be sure that all ribs are covered entirely.

6. Place the corn ribs onto the prepared baking sheet spaced about 1 inch (2.5 cm) apart and bake for 15 to 20 minutes. Ribs are done when edges start to turn golden brown. Cook for 5 to 10 minutes longer for crispier corn.

7. Once the corn ribs are done, let cool for 5 minutes before serving.

8. Serve with Spicy Creepy Crema (see page 82), or your favorite BBQ sauce.

HEED: You can also cut each ear of corn into long, thin pieces to make them look similar to their meaty counterpart! To slice into 4–8 ribs, cut off both ends of corn. With ear standing up on a cut end, slice in half lengthwise. Then lay one of these long halves cut side down and again cut in half lengthwise. (If you can manage it, cut into quarters.) Repeat with other half and remaining corn. Proceed with the recipe.

Mad Madam Mim's Cunning Coleslaw

MAKES ABOUT 8 TO 10 CUPS

Remember Madam Mim from *The Sword in the Stone* (1963)? The purple-haired witch who finds delight in the gruesome and grim? Yes, I'm talking about the one with the power-clashing outfit of magenta, maroon, and lavender. This colorful coleslaw is for her. The magic of its crunchy red cabbage, crisp sour apples, and zesty vinaigrette can bring joy to even the grumpiest, most conceited of souls.

SPECIAL EQUIPMENT NEEDED

Gallon-size plastic bag

INGREDIENTS

1 small head red cabbage, thinly sliced or julienned

1 large carrot, thinly sliced or julienned

1 Granny Smith apple, thinly sliced or julienned

3 green onions, thinly sliced

½ cup (120 ml) apple cider vinegar

2 tablespoons granulated sugar, or 1 packet sugar substitute

2 teaspoons Dijon mustard

½ teaspoon celery seed

½ teaspoon salt

½ teaspoon ground black pepper

2 tablespoons extra-virgin olive oil

1. Place the cabbage, carrot, apple, and green onions into a gallon-size (3.8 L) resealable plastic bag.

2. In a medium bowl, whisk the vinegar, sugar, mustard, celery seed, salt, pepper, and olive oil. Add the mixture to the vegetables in the bag. Close the bag and toss to combine.

3. Refrigerate for at least 1 hour. Before serving, toss again, taste, and adjust seasoning as needed.

HEED: I find mixing the coleslaw in a bag to be the best way to ensure an even coat of dressing on all ingredients. It also keeps the vegetables from getting soggy. I prefer to use a mandoline slicer for coleslaw because of its thin, clean slicing. Food processors are great for chopping, mixing, and kneading dough, but I find they cut so quickly, the sliced vegetable often ends up mushy or too wet to use. Of course, a sharp knife is an excellent option as well if you are not pressed for time.

Spooky Fruit Skewers

MAKES 15 TO 20 SKEWERS

Behold these spears of cantaloupe pumpkins, kiwi bats, blackberries, and assorted grapes. With a dash of whimsy, these skewers are a carnival for the eyes—a mishmash of colors and fruits in disguise! Destined for parties and after-school treats, these fruit assemblages defy norms, evoke chuckles, and spread spooky delight.

SPECIAL EQUIPMENT NEEDED

Mini pumpkin and bat cookie cutters, 15 to 20 bamboo skewers

INGREDIENTS

1 small cantaloupe, skin and seeds removed and cut into ½-inch (12 mm) slices

2 kiwis, peeled and cut into ½- to ¾-inch (1 to 2 cm) rounds

1 cup (225 g) seedless green grapes

1 cup (225 g) seedless red or purple grapes

¾ cup (170 g) blackberries

Red gel icing in a tube (optional)

Candy eyes (optional)

DID YOU KNOW?

Most bats don't feed on blood; they dine on fruit or insects.

1. Using a mini pumpkin cookie cutter, punch out shapes from the cantaloupe slices.

2. Using a bat cookie cutter, punch out shapes from the kiwi slices. Kiwis are fragile, so thicker slices are needed to keep bat shapes intact.

3. To assemble the skewers, use your creativity and thread cantaloupe pumpkins, kiwi bats, grapes, and blackberries onto the skewers in any order. Follow a pattern or mix it up for variety. Make sure to leave a little space at the top and bottom of the skewers for easier handling.

4. For an extra playful touch, add red gel icing dots for eyes and/or attach candy eyes to some of the fruit pieces.

5. Serve on a large tray.

HEED: Don't have mini cookie cutters? Use a melon baller or ice cream scoop. Instead of making ½-inch (12 mm) cantaloupe slices, cut the full cantaloupe in half, deseed it, and use a melon baller to scoop out melon balls. For the kiwi, remove skin and use a melon baller to create spheres or cut into circular slices.

Black Cat Magic Balls

MAKES 12 CATS

Black Cat Magic Balls are a delectable blend of oats, almond butter, chocolate, and dark cocoa. Shaped like cute cat faces, these make for a quick and satisfying snack that celebrate these mystical felines.

INGREDIENTS

1 cup (100 g) rolled oats

¼ cup (25 g) unsweetened dark cocoa powder

¼ cup (34 g) ground flaxseed

¼ cup (27 g) slivered almonds

½ cup (80 g) mini chocolate chips

2 tablespoons chia seeds

⅛ teaspoon salt

½ cup (130 g) almond butter or nut butter of choice

1 to 3 tablespoons honey, (or more if the nut butter is unsweetened)

1 teaspoon vanilla extract

1 or 2 teaspoons water or milk of choice (optional)

1 bag (8 ounces, or 227 g) dried mango slices

1 tablespoon pink mini baking chips

2 tablespoons coconut flakes

1. Line a half baking sheet with parchment paper or a non-slip silicone baking mat.

2. In a large bowl, mix the oats, cocoa powder, flaxseed, almonds, chocolate chips, chia seeds, and salt.

3. Add the almond butter, honey, and vanilla to the dry ingredients. Stir together until well combined. If the mixture is too dry, add water or milk, 1 teaspoon at a time, until the mixture comes together smoothly.

4. Using your hands, roll the mixture into bite-size balls, about a generous tablespoon. If the mixture is too gooey to form balls, refrigerate for 15 minutes; this will make it easier to roll. Place the balls on the prepared baking sheet.

5. Create ears, noses, and whiskers to turn the balls into cats. Using kitchen shears, cut the mango slices into ½-inch (12 mm) strips, then cut the strips into small equilateral triangles for the ears and place on top of the balls. If the ears will not stay, make small slits on top of the balls with a paring knife and gently nudge the mango triangles in with a toothpick. Using a toothpick, create a shallow hole for the nose and insert a pink baking chip. To create whiskers, press a pinch of coconut flakes on each side of the baking chip nose.

6. Once you have decorated all the balls, store them in an airtight container in the refrigerator for up to 5 days.

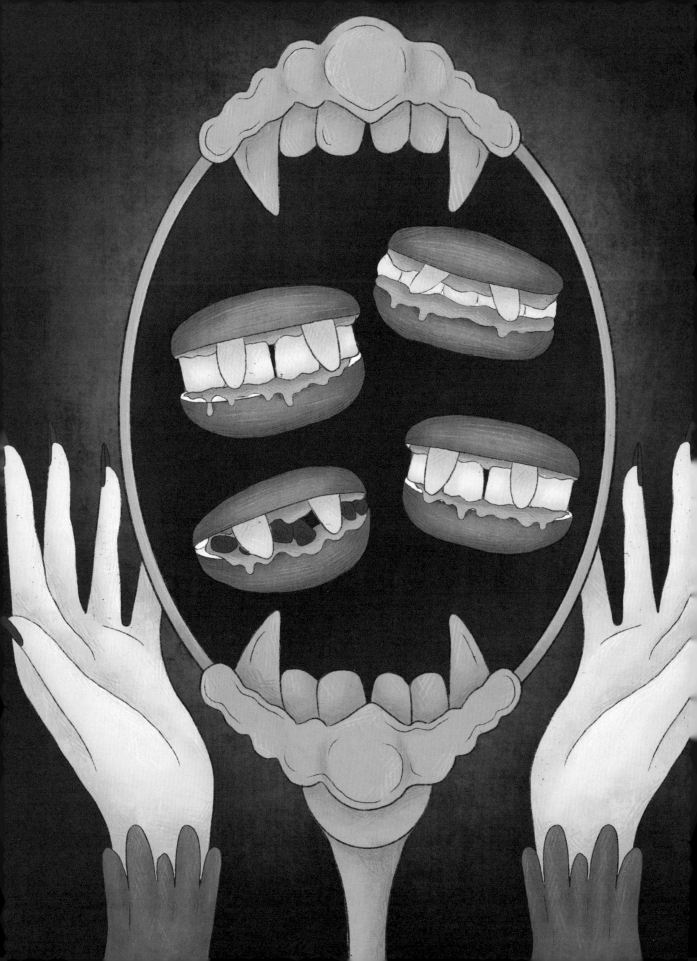

Vain Vanessa's Vampire Bites

MAKES 8 BITES

In a bewitching realm where fruit and confection collide, behold the curious creation of edible Vampire Bites. These hauntingly delightful treats of crimson-skinned apples, velvety white marshmallows, chewy black raisins, and pointy slivered almonds converge with your favorite nut butter to create a snack that smiles back. Surrender to these sweet smirks and let them cast their spell upon you!

SPECIAL EQUIPMENT NEEDED

Apple corer

INGREDIENTS

1 apple, red varieties work best

1 tablespoon lemon juice

¼ cup (65 g) peanut butter or nut butter of choice

¼ cup (15 g) mini marshmallows

2 tablespoons raisins

¼ cup (27 g) slivered almonds or sunflower seeds

1. Using an apple corer, remove the core of the apple. Cut the apple into quarters, then cut each quarter in half to make 8 slices total.

2. Combine the lemon juice and 2 tablespoons of water. Brush this mixture onto the apple slices to prevent browning.

3. Cut an apple slice in half lengthwise to form the upper and lower lips of a smiling mouth.

4. Spread some peanut butter on one of these lips, then place marshmallows and/or raisins in a line along the slice rim.

5. On the other half slice, create vampire fangs by poking the slivered almonds into the apple, close to the edge. If the almonds break, use a sharp knife tip to make a shallow hole to insert the almond. Place two slivered almonds in a row, add extra marshmallow or raisin teeth– use your imagination for all kinds of chilling grins. Then spread peanut butter on this slice and set atop other apple half to create vampire bite.

6. Serve these toothy smiles on a platter and enjoy!

DID YOU KNOW?

According to legend, a vampire's elongated canine teeth, or fangs, enable them to not only feed from tasty necks, but also sense desirable blood types from a distance, intimidate opponents, and transform victims into vampires themselves.

Dr. Frankenstein's Monster Mash

MAKES 4 MONSTERS

Be warned: This dish is so delicious that it may have a life of its own! When you gaze upon the lumpy green flesh of this monstrosity, you'll feel uneasy as well as a little hungry. It will be as if the very essence of Dr. Frankenstein's experiment has been distilled into this humble little snack. And yet, despite its unsettling appearance, you'll be drawn into the complex interplay of creamy avocado, salty seasonings, and savory hash browns. Maybe you've unlocked the secrets of creation . . . or maybe you just have an empty stomach.

INGREDIENTS

4 frozen hash brown patties

2 ripe Haas avocados

1 package (12-pack) seaweed snack, seasoned with sea salt

2 to 3 tablespoons everything bagel seasoning, for topping

1. Preheat the oven to 400°F (205°C, or gas mark 6) and place the hash browns in a single layer on a baking sheet lined with parchment paper. Bake for 15 to 20 minutes, turning halfway through, until extra crispy and golden brown.

2. Cut the avocados in half, remove the pits, and scoop out the flesh into a small bowl. Mash the flesh with a fork or potato masher until creamy.

3. Using kitchen shears or scissors, cut out triangle eyes, noses, toothy grins, spiky hair, and whiskers from the seaweed sheets.

4. Spread creamy avocado on top of each hash brown, then generously sprinkle with the everything bagel seasoning.

5. Arrange the seaweed cutouts atop avocado spread to create Frankenstein, jack-o'-lantern, and ghost faces.

HEED: Did someone forget to stock the lab with everything bagel seasoning? No problem, just create your own. Mix together 1 teaspoon of each: white sesame seeds, dried minced onion, dried minced garlic, black sesame seeds, sea salt flakes or coarse salt, and poppy seeds. Stir until well combined. Store in an airtight container.

Pseudo Snickers from Outer Space

MAKES 12 SNICKERS

Pseudo Snickers definitely come from an otherworldly place. Your mind will think these chewy, crunchy, and sweet snack-size treats are your favorite candy bar, but really they are a Tik Tok–inspired, nutrient-dense snack that are high in fiber and loaded with potassium, magnesium, and antioxidants. You'll really be confused when you see them smiling back at you.

SPECIAL EQUIPMENT NEEDED

Bento food picks, eye-style

INGREDIENTS

12 Medjool dates

¼ cup (55 g) creamy peanut butter, divided

¼ cup (35 g) dry roasted peanuts, separated into halves, plus crushed peanuts for topping

1 cup (190 g) semisweet chocolate chips

2 teaspoons coconut oil

1 to 2 tablespoons flaky salt

HEED: These treats are delicious if peanuts are switched out for any other nut or nut butter combination. The same goes for replacing semisweet chocolate chips with dark chocolate or vegan chocolate chips.

1. Place a sheet of parchment paper or a non-slip silicone baking mat in a roomy plastic container or on a half baking sheet that can be placed in the freezer.

2. Slice each date lengthwise and spread it open like a butterfly. Remove seeds if necessary.

3. Spoon about 1 teaspoon of peanut butter into each date, adding more if needed.

4. Insert 3 to 5 peanut halves into one side of each date. (These are the creature's "teeth.") Then fold closed like a taco and secure with a toothpick, vertically.

5. Combine the chocolate chips and coconut oil in a medium microwaveable bowl. Microwave in 30-second intervals, stirring after each interval, until just melted and smooth. Be careful not to overheat the chocolate as it can burn easily.

6. Holding a date by its toothpick, dip it into the melted chocolate, avoiding the peanut area. Use a spoon to help coat evenly. Let any excess chocolate drip off.

7. Place dates in the prepared container or tray. Sprinkle with flaky salt and crushed peanuts.

8. Place in freezer for 30 minutes to set chocolate. Remove toothpicks and insert eye-style food picks into the holes that were left.

Rickety Old Pretzel Bones

MAKES 16 BONES

The sight of bones can be jarring or unsettling, particularly if they are presented out of context or in a way that emphasizes their shape or structure . . . exactly why these chewy, homemade pretzels are an excellently spooky treat.

SPECIAL EQUIPMENT NEEDED

Stand mixer with whisk attachment

INGREDIENTS

2¼ teaspoons active dry yeast (1 packet)

1 tablespoon granulated sugar

1½ cups (360 ml) warm water

2 tablespoons olive oil or melted butter, plus more for greasing dough bowl

4 cups (500 g) all-purpose flour, plus more for dusting

1 teaspoon salt

Cooking oil spray

1 egg, beaten, for egg wash

1 tablespoon milk of choice, for egg wash

Coarse or kosher salt, for topping

2 tablespoons butter, melted, for topping

Mustard or nacho cheese dip, for serving

1. In the bowl of a stand mixer with the whisk attachment, combine the yeast, sugar, and warm water. Let rest until mixture starts bubbling, 5 to 10 minutes.

2. Add the olive oil, flour, and salt to the yeast mixture. Switch attachment to dough hook and mix on low for 2 minutes, or until mixture is combined. Scrape down sides if needed. Increase speed to medium, and mix until dough is smooth, elastic, and no longer sticks to the side of the bowl, 5 to 7 minutes. (If dough is still sticky, continue to mix).

3. Place the dough in a large, greased bowl. Cover with plastic wrap or a kitchen towel and let it rise in a warm place for about 1 hour, or until it has doubled in size.

4. Preheat the oven to 450°F (230°C, or gas mark 8). Line 2 half baking sheets with parchment paper or a non-slip silicone baking mat and spray with cooking oil.

5. Turn dough out on a flour-dusted surface. Roll dough into a 15-inch (38 cm) log, and then divide into 16 equal pieces.

6. Roll and stretch each piece of dough into a rope about 13 to 15 inches (33 to 38 cm) long. Tie a loose basic knot at each dough end. Place on the prepared baking sheets so tops of knots are facing down.

7. In a small bowl, mix together the beaten egg and milk to make an egg wash. Brush each unbaked bone with egg wash, making sure to evenly coat. The egg wash will help the salt to stick.

8. Sprinkle each pretzel with salt. Bake for 10 to 14 minutes, until tops are golden brown. Carefully watch bottoms to prevent burning.

9. Remove from the oven and drizzle with the melted butter. Serve the bones warm with mustard or nacho cheese dip.

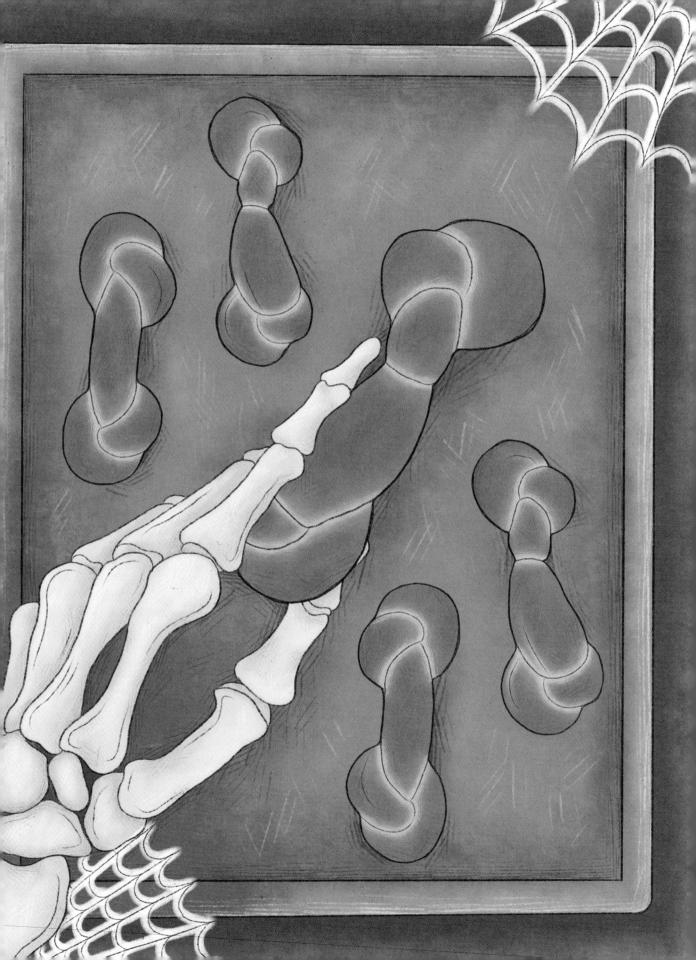

 Monstrous Main Dishes

Get ready for a bloodthirsty swarm of macabre main attractions! Preternatural dishes of carnivorous delights and plant-based sorcery that will please any ravenous blur of teeth and tentacles. Perfect for hectic moonless nights and wicked weekends, these hearty creations promise to keep your meals creepy, speedy, and hit the spot. Showpieces of snaggle-toothed pumpkins, possessed pork sandwiches, and pasta that gives you the stink eye are easy to make and devilishly delicious. So put on your pointiest witch's hat, tend to your cauldron, and conjure these recipes to subdue your famished flock.

Apple Cider-Glazed Chicken

MAKES 4 CHICKEN BREASTS

This dish is a tribute to fall's arrival, a reminder that in its flavors, we find solace and comfort as nature transitions.

SPECIAL EQUIPMENT NEEDED

Plastic wrap, meat mallet, large skillet or fry pan

INGREDIENTS

CHICKEN

4 chicken breasts, boneless, skinless

2 tablespoons olive oil, plus more for cooking, if needed

1 to 2 tablespoons soup stock, if needed to thin sauce

MARINADE

1 cup (240 ml) apple cider

⅓ cup (75 ml) extra-virgin olive oil

2 tablespoons apple cider vinegar

3 tablespoons honey

1 teaspoon Worcestershire sauce

¼ cup (60 ml) soy sauce

1 teaspoon chopped fresh rosemary (½ teaspoon dried)

1 teaspoon chopped fresh thyme (½ teaspoon dried)

4 cloves garlic, minced

2 teaspoons salt

½ teaspoon ground black pepper

1. Rinse the chicken and pat it dry. Place the chicken between plastic wrap and gently pound from center outward with a meat mallet or heavy pan. Check for uniform thinness. Remove the wrap and place the chicken into a plastic bag.

2. To make the marinade: Whisk together the apple cider, olive oil, apple cider vinegar, honey, Worcestershire sauce, soy sauce, rosemary, thyme, garlic, salt, and pepper in a medium bowl.

3. Pour the marinade into the plastic bag containing the chicken, press out the air, and seal. Marinate in the refrigerator overnight.

4. Remove the chicken from the marinade, shake off the excess, and pat dry. Set the marinade aside. In a large skillet over medium-high heat, heat the olive oil until hot. Add the chicken and cook for 5 to 9 minutes, until the chicken is golden brown and releases easily from the pan. If the pan is crowded with all 4 chicken breasts, cook in 2 batches and add more oil when needed.

5. Brush the chicken with the remaining olive oil and then flip. Cook for 3 to 6 minutes more, until its internal temperature reaches 165°F (74°C).

6. When done, remove the chicken and set aside. Cook the remaining chicken breasts if needed.

7. With the heat still on, add the remaining marinade to an empty skillet and bring to a rolling boil for 5 minutes, or until the temperature reaches 165°F (74°C). (You want to make sure any bacteria is killed off.) Continue to cook for 5 to 10 minutes, until the marinade reduces into a thick sauce. (If it gets too thick, add 1 to 2 tablespoons of water or soup stock to thin it.)

8. Serve the chicken breasts topped with sauce or place the sauce on the side in a small bowl. Enjoy!

Attack of the Killer Tomato Soup

MAKES 2 TO 4 SERVINGS

Attack of the Killer Tomatoes (1978) is a comedic horror film in which gigantic mutant tomatoes attack and kill people. So bad it's funny, the film will make you side-eye fresh tomatoes and question the contents of most tomato soups. . . but not this tomato soup. Jazzed up with aromatics and absolutely no ingredients from failed government experiments, this tomato soup recipe is a masterpiece of what you'll want to believe are simple ingredients and delicious flavors. Serve it with Chilling Cheddar Puff Pastries (see page 153), to give a flaky layered spin to the classic grilled cheese and tomato soup pairing.

SPECIAL EQUIPMENT NEEDED

Soup pot, immersion blender

INGREDIENTS

2 tablespoons olive oil

1 large onion, diced

1 medium carrot, diced

2 tablespoons tomato paste

2 cloves garlic, minced

1 can (28 ounces, or 794 g) fire-roasted tomatoes

½ teaspoon salt

¼ teaspoon ground black pepper

½ teaspoon dried thyme

1 teaspoon Italian seasoning

2 cups (480 ml) soup stock or broth

½ teaspoon red pepper flakes (optional)

1 teaspoon granulated sugar (optional)

1. In a large pot over medium heat, add the olive oil.

2. Once the oil is hot, sauté the onion and carrot until translucent, about 5 minutes.

3. Add the tomato paste and garlic. Cook for another minute, until fragrant.

4. Add the tomatoes, salt, pepper, and herbs and stir. Let simmer for 10 to 15 minutes, stirring often.

5. Pour in the stock and stir. Add the red pepper flakes and sugar. Taste and adjust the seasoning. Turn off the heat. Carefully purée with the immersion blender until smooth.

6. Serve warm and enjoy!

Ginger Shrimp for the Recently Deceased

MAKES 3 TO 4 SERVINGS

In the ghoulish world of *Beetlejuice* (1988), the afterlife is anything but ordinary and a freelance bio-exorcist may be an answer to your problems. Enter this flavorful ginger soy shrimp and noodle dish with a quick and delicious Asian-inspired sauce that will tell your taste buds it's showtime!

SPECIAL EQUIPMENT NEEDED

Large skillet

INGREDIENTS

2 tablespoons soy sauce

3 tablespoons rice vinegar

1½ teaspoons fresh ginger, minced

2 cloves garlic, minced

2 teaspoons brown sugar

1 tablespoon sesame oil

1 pound (454 g) raw medium shrimp, peeled, deveined, and butterflied

½ cup (120 ml) broth

1 teaspoon cornstarch

½ cup (115 g) rice noodles

2 tablespoons vegetable oil

1 cup (225 g) frozen edamame, shelled, room temperature

4 green onions, minced

Hot chili sauce (such as Sriracha), to add heat and/or garnish (optional)

1. In a small bowl, combine the soy sauce, rice vinegar, ginger, garlic, brown sugar, and sesame oil. Mix well until the brown sugar is fully dissolved.

2. Pat the shrimp dry with paper towels. Place the shrimp in a bowl or a zip-top bag and pour in about half of the mixture. Seal the bag and toss to coat the shrimp evenly. Let marinate for about 15 minutes.

3. Whisk broth and cornstarch into the remaining marinade. Set aside.

4. Boil a pot of water and prepare rice noodles according to package directions. Drain and set aside.

5. In a large skillet over medium-high heat, add the vegetable oil. Once hot, add the marinated shrimp in a single layer. Cook for 1 to 2 minutes per side, until they turn pink and opaque. Be careful not to overcook them; shrimp cooks quickly. Remove from the heat and transfer to a serving bowl.

6. Pour the remaining marinade sauce and edamame into the skillet and stir well. Simmer until sauce thickens. Remove the skillet from the heat. Add cooked rice noodles and cooked shrimp. Stir to incorporate.

7. Top with green onions. Serve while hot with some hot chili sauce, if you like.

HEED: To butterfly shrimp, use a paring knife to make a shallow cut along the curved side of each shrimp. Take care not to cut all the way through. Gently press the shrimp open, creating a butterfly shape. This technique enhances flavor and allows for even cooking.

Phases of the Moon Hand Pies

MAKES 8 PIES

The moon's phases can spawn crazy behavior. With these empanada-inspired creations, you will be ready to embrace the lunacy of it all.

SPECIAL EQUIPMENT NEEDED

Large heavy-bottomed skillet or sauté pan, pastry brush

INGREDIENTS

FILLING

2 tablespoons vegetable oil

1 small onion, finely chopped

2 cloves garlic, minced

1 cup (150 g) sweet potatoes, peeled and diced into bite-size cubes

¼ cup (60 ml) broth, divided

Salt and ground black pepper

1 cup (198 g) lentils, cooked and drained

1 teaspoon ground cumin

1 teaspoon smoked paprika

¼ teaspoon ground cinnamon

¼ teaspoon ground ginger

¼ cup (34 g) green olives, pitted and diced

¼ cup (55 g) dates, pitted and finely diced

HAND PIES

2 cans (8 ounces, or 227 g) crescent roll dough

Flour, for dusting

1 egg, beaten, for egg wash

1 teaspoon heavy cream or milk of choice, for egg wash

1. To make the filling: Heat the vegetable oil in a large skillet or sauté pan over medium-high heat. Add the onion, garlic, and sweet potatoes. Add 2 tablespoons of broth. Sprinkle with salt and pepper. Stir well. Cover and cook, stirring often, for about 5 minutes.

2. Turn the heat down to medium. Uncover, stir, and continue to cook the potatoes another 5 minutes, or until they are lightly browned. Add the lentils, cumin, paprika, cinnamon, and ginger. Stir well and cook for 5 minutes, or until the spices are fragrant and well incorporated. If the mixture is dry, add 2 additional tablespoons of broth at a time and stir to incorporate. The mixture should be moist. Remove from the heat. Stir in the olives and dates. Taste and adjust the seasoning.

3. To make the hand pies: Preheat the oven to 375°F (190°C, or gas mark 5). Line a baking sheet with parchment paper.

4. Following the package directions, open the tube and separate the crescent roll dough into 4 rectangles. Firmly pinch together any perforations on the dough to seal them. Sprinkle with flour. Using a rolling pin, roll the dough into 4 × 8 inch (10 × 20 cm) rectangles.

5. Place 2 tablespoons of the filling onto each piece of dough. Fold the dough in half and shape into a moon phase (see page 147 for guidance). Seal the dough edges together by crimping with a fork or twisting to create a rope-like edge. Place on the baking sheet.

6. Repeat with the remaining dough and second tube of crescent roll dough to create the 8 phases of the moon.

7. In a small bowl, whisk together the egg and heavy cream or milk. Using a pastry brush, brush each pie to cover with egg wash.

8. Bake for 12 to 20 minutes, until golden brown. Arrange into moon phases, from Waxing Crescent to Waning Crescent, and serve.

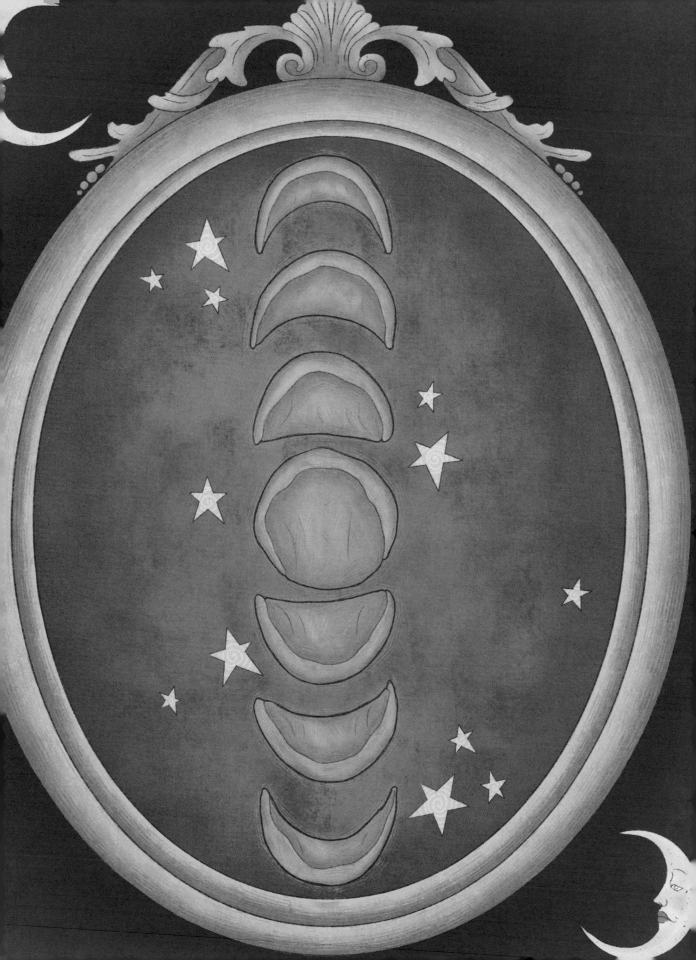

Stuffed Pepper Jack-O'-Lanterns

MAKES 6 JACK-O'-LANTERNS

Jack-o'-lanterns are delightful decorations that instantly broadcast "Halloween is here!" Usually seen in seasonal displays on doorsteps and windowsills, these Stuffed Pepper Jack-O'-Lanterns now bring the spirit of the season to your dinner plate. Their sweet smiles hold a savory combination of flavorful filling and tender, roasted pepper. Easy to make, tasty to eat, and lovely to look at, Stuffed Pepper Jack-O'-Lanterns are a playful spin-off of this well-known dish.

INGREDIENTS

6 orange, red, and yellow bell peppers, tops, cores, and seeds removed

2 tablespoons olive oil

1 small onion, diced

½ pound (227 g) ground beef

½ pound (227 g) ground sausage

Salt and ground black pepper, to taste

3 cloves garlic, minced

1½ cups (318 g) black rice, cooked

1 can (15 ounce, or 425 g) diced tomatoes

1½ teaspoons Italian seasoning

¼ cup (29 g) fontina cheese, sliced into 6 pieces

1½ cup (173 g) shredded fontina cheese

1. Preheat the oven to 350°F (175°C, or gas mark 4) and grease a 9 × 13 inch (23 × 33 cm) casserole dish.

2. It's time to carve the jack-o'-lanterns! Use a sharp paring knife to carefully cut out eyes, a nose, and a mouth on the front side of each pepper. Position faces between the capsaicin glands (white strips on the inside of the pepper) for cleaner cuts. Get creative and make different expressions for each one. If a pepper does not sit upright, slice some of the bottom off, making sure to not cut into the pepper cavity. When done carving, place the pepper in the casserole dish.

3. To make the stuffing: Heat the oil in a skillet over medium-high heat. Add the onion. Cook for 5 minutes, or until the onion is softened. Add the beef and sausage and cook until browned, 5 to 6 minutes. Season with salt and pepper.

4. Add the garlic and cook for 30 seconds, or until aromatic. Remove the skillet from the heat and add the cooked rice, can of tomatoes (including juice), and Italian seasoning. Stir to combine.

5. To create an oozing effect: Place a slice of cheese against the inside of each carved face side, then fill the peppers with the stuffing. Gently press the mixture down to fill the entire pepper.

6. Top with the shredded cheese and bake uncovered for 35 to 40 minutes, until the cheese is melted and the peppers are soft. Remove from the oven and let cool slightly before serving. Carved faces should be visible, cute, and spooky.

Pulled Pork Poltergeist Sandwiches

MAKES 6 TO 8 SANDWICHES

Poltergeist activity can include a range of strange occurrences such as unexplained noises, objects moving or being thrown . . . and a delicious meal prepared without a lot of work and time in the kitchen. Let's not question it too closely. This is an excellent meal to serve post trick-or-treating.

SPECIAL EQUIPMENT NEEDED

Slow cooker/Pressure cooker with slow cooker setting, Bento food picks, eye-style

INGREDIENTS

2½ pounds (1.1 kg) pork shoulder

2 cups (480 ml) ketchup

1 medium onion, finely chopped

⅓ cup (75 ml) apple cider vinegar

¼ cup (60 ml) honey

¼ cup (60 ml) tomato paste

2 tablespoons smoked paprika

1 tablespoon soy sauce

1 teaspoon hot sauce, optional

2 teaspoons salt

½ teaspoon ground black pepper

½ teaspoon chili powder

1 teaspoon garlic powder

6 to 8 brioche burger buns, toasted and buttered

12 to 16 green olives with pimentos, for garnish

1 whole dill pickle, thinly sliced lengthwise, for garnish

1. Remove any string or netting from the pork shoulder and wipe clean with a paper towel. Cut the roast in half for faster cooking and more exposure to the sauce while cooking.

2. In a slow cooker, combine all the ingredients except the roast, buns, and garnishes, and stir.

3. Add the pork pieces. Stir well, making sure to completely cover the roast in sauce.

4. Cover the slow cooker and cook for 6 to 8 hours on low (or the normal setting on Instapot). The roast is done when it is tender and easily pulled apart with a fork. Check the internal temperature about 1 hour before it is done and adjust the cooking time as needed. The internal temperature should be at least 145°F (63°C).

5. Transfer the roast to a cutting board and let rest for 15 minutes. Using a knife or two forks, shred the roast, pulling it apart along the grain. Discard any excess fat or bones. Place the shreds back into the slow cooker pot and stir to incorporate with sauce. Then spoon the mixture directly onto brioche buns.

6. To create monster faces: Be inspired by the poltergeist's unexplainable and disruptive nature! Place the olives on toothpicks or use eye-style food picks for eyes, sliced dill pickle for tongues, and carrots and cabbage from coleslaw as pointy teeth, weird whiskers, horns, and hair.

7. Serve with Mad Madam Mim's Cunning Coleslaw (see page 48).

Frightening Chicken Fingers

MAKES 4 SERVINGS

For a spine-chilling, creepy meal, create chicken tenders that resemble severed ogre fingers! Start by sculpting chicken tenders into finger-like shapes. Dip them in seasoned flour and an egg wash. Then coat the fingers in a creepy crust made from Italian-style breadcrumbs and Parmesan. Fry on the stovetop until crispy and arrange on a serving platter, adding almonds as pointy talons for that sinister touch. Present these frightening fingers to your unsuspecting guests for a truly ghoulish dining experience that will send shivers down their spines (and fingers). Bon(e) appétit!

SPECIAL EQUIPMENT NEEDED

Medium pan or iron skillet

INGREDIENTS

¼ cup (33 g) all-purpose flour

½ teaspoon salt

¼ teaspoon ground black pepper

1 teaspoon paprika

1 large egg, beaten, for egg wash

½ teaspoon hot sauce, or more for hotter spice level, for egg wash

⅓ cup (40 g) finely shredded Parmesan cheese

½ cup (58 g) seasoned-breadcrumbs (or plain breadcrumbs mixed with 1 tablespoon Italian seasoning)

1 pound (454 g) boneless, skinless chicken tenders

2 tablespoons vegetable oil, or more to evenly coat bottom of pan or skillet

⅓ cup (45 g) whole almonds

1. In a small bowl or on a plate, combine the flour, salt, pepper, and paprika. Stir well.

2. In a separate small bowl, whisk together the egg and hot sauce until well combined.

3. In a third bowl, stir the Parmesan and breadcrumbs.

4. Dip each chicken finger into the flour mixture, coating it evenly. Shake off any excess flour.

5. Next, dip the floured chicken finger into the egg wash, allowing any excess to drip off.

6. Roll the chicken finger in the breadcrumb mixture, pressing lightly to ensure the breadcrumbs adhere well. Repeat the process for each piece of chicken.

7. In a medium iron skillet or pan over medium-high heat, add the oil. Once the oil heats up, about 2 minutes, add the chicken tenders.

8. Cook the chicken tenders for 5 minutes on one side and then flip to other side. Cook for an additional 5 minutes, or until chicken is cooked through and reaches an internal temperature of 165°F (74°C). Remove the tenders from the skillet or pan and place them on paper towels to absorb any excess oil. While still warm, make a shallow lateral slice about ½ to 1 inch (1 to 3 cm) on the end of each chicken tender to make a small flap. Work 1 almond into each pocket to create an almond fingernail.

9. Serve the chicken fingers hot with your favorite dipping sauces, such as ketchup, barbecue sauce, honey mustard, or ranch dressing.

Cyclops Cy's Spaghetti Nests

MAKES 6 TO 10 NESTS

From a faraway land without law and order, these nests take a whimsical and cheesy twist on classic baked spaghetti.

SPECIAL EQUIPMENT NEEDED
Immersion blender or food processor

INGREDIENTS
SAUCE
2 pounds (900 g) Roma tomatoes, halved

2 shallots, peeled and cut in quarters

4 tablespoons olive oil, divided

½ teaspoon dried thyme

½ teaspoon garlic powder

¾ teaspoon salt, plus more to taste

¼ teaspoon ground black pepper, plus more to taste

½ teaspoon red pepper flakes (optional)

1 pound (454 g) ground beef

1 small onion, chopped

SPAGHETTI NESTS
Cooking oil spray

3 eggs, beaten

3 tablespoons heavy cream

¼ cup (30 g) shredded Parmesan cheese

1 box (7.05 ounces, or 200 g) black soybean spaghetti, cooked

8 ounces (227 g) bocconcini (small mozzarella balls)

3 to 5 kalamata olives, thinly sliced into circles

2 or 3 very thin slices roasted red pepper

1. To make the sauce: Preheat the oven to 375°F (190°C, or gas mark 5) and line a half baking sheet with parchment paper.

2. In a large bowl, combine the tomatoes, shallots, 3 tablespoons of olive oil, thyme, garlic powder, salt, pepper, and red pepper flakes. Spread the mixture onto the baking sheet, with the tomatoes cut side down. Bake for 45 minutes, or until the tomatoes begin to shrivel and soften.

3. Heat the remaining oil in a large skillet over medium-high heat. Add the ground beef and onion. Season with salt and pepper. Cook for 7 to 10 minutes, stirring constantly, until browned. Drain off the excess grease.

4. In a large bowl, purée the roasted tomato mixture with the immersion blender or wait for the mixture to cool and purée in a food processor. Add the tomato purée to the beef, stir, and bring to a low simmer over medium-low heat. Keep sauce warm while you make the nests.

5. To make the spaghetti nests: Preheat the oven to 375°F (190°C, or gas mark 5). Grease a 9" x 13" (23 cm x 33 cm) casserole dish with cooking oil spray.

6. In a large bowl, whisk together the eggs, heavy cream, and Parmesan. Add the cooked spaghetti and toss well. Using a large fork and your hands, twist the spaghetti into nests and place into the casserole dish. Bake for 15 to 20 minutes.

7. To compose the nests: Spoon ¼ cup (60 ml) of sauce onto a serving plate and place a nest on top. Nestle one bocconcini into the middle. Top with an olive iris and thin (½-inch, or 1.3 cm long) red pepper blood vessels.

Merv Mummy's Posthumous Pizza

MAKES 6 MUMMIES

Do mummies enjoy pizza? *Of corpse!* This recipe unwraps quickly to add some spooky flair to your pizza night. Use pitted olives, cooked sausage, or your favorite pizza topping to mimic a 4,000-year-old vacant stare, a contorted eternal scream of pain, or any number of unique facial features.

INGREDIENTS

1 loaf Italian bread

2 tablespoons spreadable butter

½ teaspoon garlic powder

1 can or jar (14 ounces, or 396 g) pizza sauce of choice

1 package (6 ounce, or 170 g) sliced pepperoni or other pizza toppings of choice (optional)

12 mozzarella string cheese sticks, whole milk preferred

6 to 8 pitted black olives

1. Preheat the oven to 400°F (205°C, or gas mark 6). Line a half baking sheet with parchment paper or foil for easy cleanup.

2. Slice the bread into 3 sections, then slice each section in half lengthwise.

3. On each piece of bread, spread butter, sprinkle with garlic powder, and spread 2 to 3 tablespoons of pizza sauce. If using, add the pepperoni and other desired toppings.

4. Unwrap the string cheese sticks. (Keeping them cold will make the cheese easier to slice.) Using a vegetable peeler, slice each stick lengthwise to create mummy wraps. Slice as much of each stick as possible. Cheese will be jagged, messy, and uneven, just like the wrappings of an ancient mummy.

5. Weave the cheese strips in a crisscross pattern on top of the bread to create the appearance of bandages. Make sure to leave room for the eyes!

6. Vertically slice the pitted olives into 3 circles. Use 2 circles to create hollow eyes. Roll a tiny piece of cheese into a ball and place it in the olive's center to make the eyes pop. Add a third olive circle for a silently screaming mouth.

7. Place on the baking sheet and bake the mummies for 8 to 10 minutes. Briefly cool and enjoy.

HEED: These pizza mummies can be made as small or large as you like. Simply adjust the size of your bread slices to create fewer or more individual servings.

Murder Is Like Black Bean Tacos

MAKES 10 TACOS

A certain king of horror author might have said something like, "Murder is like black bean tacos; you can't stop with just one." He would definitely say this or something similar after chowing down on several of these delicious and intensely flavorful palate pleasers. For the crispiest tacos, serve right after frying.

SPECIAL EQUIPMENT NEEDED

Potato masher or immersion blender

INGREDIENTS

SPICY CREEPY CREMA

⅓ cup (77 g) mayonnaise

1 teaspoon hot chili sauce (such as Sriracha)

1½ teaspoons lime juice

2 tablespoons unsweetened milk of choice

1 tablespoon ranch dressing

TACOS

1 can (14 ounces, or 400 g) black beans

½ teaspoon garlic powder

½ teaspoon onion powder

½ teaspoon chili powder

½ teaspoon ground cumin

½ teaspoon salt

10 fajita-style flour tortillas (6 inches, or 15 cm)

1 cup (250 g) pumpkin purée

1 cup (115 g) shredded Cheddar cheese

1 cup (115 g) shredded Monterey Jack cheese

4 to 5 tablespoons vegetable oil

1. To prepare the Spicy Creepy Crema: In a medium bowl, whisk together the mayonnaise, hot chili sauce, lime juice, unsweetened milk, and ranch dressing. Adjust the flavors to your liking and refrigerate until ready to use.

2. To make the tacos: Drain the black beans and transfer to a large bowl. Add the garlic powder, onion powder, chili powder, cumin, and salt and mix well. Using a potato masher or an immersion blender, mash or purée the beans until smooth. If the beans are hard, microwave in 30-second increments to soften.

3. Spread about 1½ tablespoons bean mixture on one side of each tortilla and about 1 tablespoon of pumpkin purée on the other half. Sprinkle with about 1½ tablespoons of each cheese and fold over, making sure the edges are sealed.

4. In a medium skillet, heat 1 tablespoon oil over medium heat. Pan-fry 2 tacos at a time on one side for 2 minutes, or until golden. Flip and cook the other sides of the tacos for 1 minute, or until golden. Repeat with the remaining oil and tacos. You may need to adjust the heat to avoid burning as the pan will get hotter.

5. Serve warm with Spicy Creepy Crema.

HEED: If the tortillas crack when folded, make them more pliable by popping them in the microwave for 10 to 20 seconds.

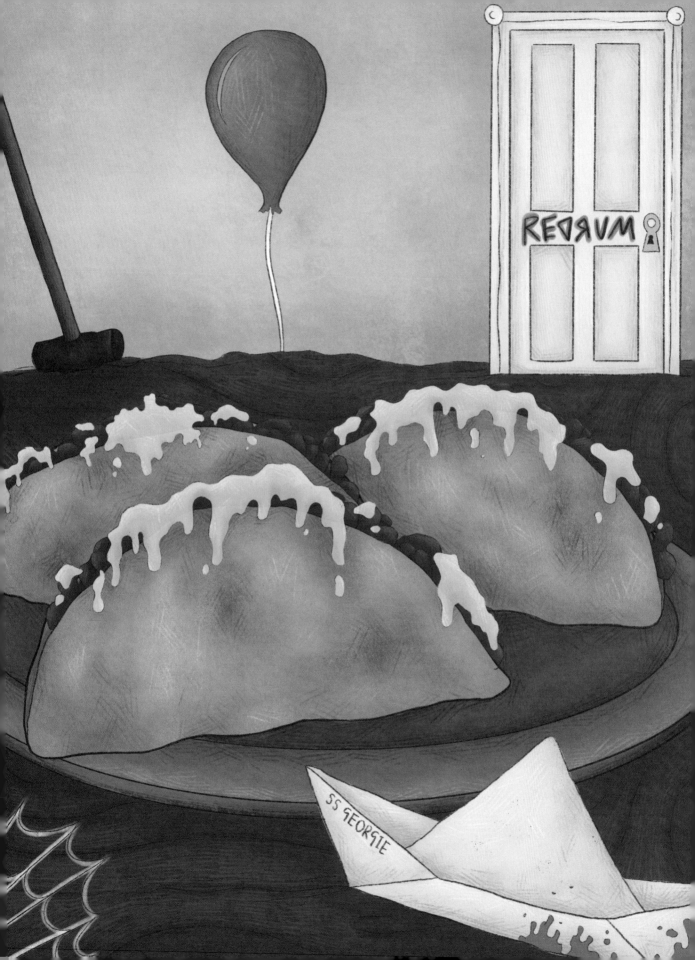

Sinister Sweets & Diabolical Desserts

When phantom footsteps follow you and spookish specters loom around every corner, sweets and desserts can be your sanctuary! Serpentine confections slither across your plate while mysterious spell books weave more than just a hex. Perfect for an office mummy mixer, a best friend boo bash, or a spooktacular school soirée, these treats are imaginative twists on beloved classics. Guaranteed to satisfy even the stinkiest, pukiest, rottenest, yuckiest of monsters.

Freaky Treat Feast Snack Board

MAKES 30 CANDY CORN FRUIT SNACKS, 12 HATS, AND 12 EYES

This Halloween-themed dessert platter of candy corn fruit snacks, peanut butter cup witch hats, and sandwich cookie eyeballs will tame any monster's munchies.

INGREDIENTS

1 can (20 ounces, or 567 g) pineapple rings, or about 10 rings

1 can (15 ounces, or 425 g) pear slices, or about 10 slices

1 can (15 ounces, or 425 g) peach slices, or about 15 slices

6 packages (1.5 ounces, or 42 g) peanut butter chocolate candies (such as Reese's Peanut Butter Cups) (12 cups), unwrapped

3 tubes writing icing: green, red, yellow

12 chocolate candies (such as Hershey's Kisses), unwrapped

12 star-shaped candy sprinkles

1 package (13.3 ounces, or 377 g) chocolate sandwich cookies (such as Oreos)

12 eye candies

1 bag (7 ounces, or 198 g) sweet and salty or kettle corn popcorn

1 bag (12 ounces, or 340 g) mini pretzels

1. To make the candy corn fruit snacks: Cut each pineapple ring and pear slice into thirds. Then cut each peach slice in half crosswise. You should have 30 pieces of each fruit.

2. Working bottom to top, mimic the stripes of candy corn with fruit slices by stacking a white piece of pineapple, an orange piece of peach, and then a white pear piece, lining up each edge.

3. Cut each fruit group into a triangle shape. Slip the toothpick through all three segments.

4. To make the witch hats: Place the peanut butter chocolate candies upside down on a baking sheet. Using a tube of green writing icing, pipe a circle of icing on the cup and place a chocolate candy on top. Press the candy down so the icing squishes out along the edges to give the appearance of a hat band. Place the candy star along the icing band to make a buckle. Let sit for 30 minutes, or until the icing hardens. Place the baking sheet in the refrigerator for faster cooling.

5. To make the sandwich cookie eyeballs: Separate 12 chocolate sandwich cookies, making sure the cream layer on one cookie is intact. Discard (or eat!) the cookie wafers without the cream. On the cream side of the cookie wafer, use red icing to create lines that radiate from the center of the cookie and yellow icing to add highlights. Pipe a green icing circle and place a candy eye in the center. Let sit for 30 minutes, or until the icing hardens.

6. To assemble the board: Stack the candy corn fruit snacks on a small plate and place in the middle of the board. (This will prevent any fruit juice making the other treats soggy.) Then group witch hats on the upper left of the snack board, and cookie eyeballs on the lower right. Fill empty spaces with popcorn and pretzels. Serve as is, or add plastic spiders and small pumpkins, for a festive touch.

Candy Spiderwebs

MAKES 12 SPIDERWEBS

Behold the confectionery enigma of webs spun from white chocolate. These candy webs may not ensnare live insects, but they do attract the unknowing sweet tooth of soon-to-be prey.

INGREDIENTS

1 bag (16 ounces, or 454 g) pretzel sticks (about 50 sticks total)

1 cup (170 g) white chocolate chips

12 spider-shaped sprinkles

Sugar pearl sprinkles, for dusting

White sparkling sugar, for dusting

1. Line a baking sheet with parchment paper or a non-slip silicone baking mat.

2. Break 3 pretzel sticks in half. Using the 6 halves, create a radiating star, with the broken ends of the pretzel sticks facing inward. Place the ends close together so a small open circle forms in the center. Continue using groups of 3 pretzel sticks to create uneven and off-kilter webs, as seen in nature.

3. Place the white chocolate in a microwavable bowl and microwave on defrost setting or at 50 percent for 1 minute. Stir thoroughly until the bowl is no longer warm. Continue to microwave at the same setting in 15- to 30-second intervals, stirring until the chocolate is almost completely melted.

4. Using a spatula, scrape the white chocolate into a sandwich-size plastic bag. Cut a tiny tip from a bottom corner of the bag and squeeze the chocolate down in preparation for piping.

5. Beginning in the center of each pretzel group, create a circle of white chocolate to hold the pretzel sticks together.

6. Drizzle the white chocolate around the pretzel sticks in increasingly larger circles to make lines that look like a sticky web of spider silk.

7. Once all the spiderwebs are created, make a small dab of white chocolate on each web and place a spider-shaped sprinkle. Create spider egg sacs by placing a group of sugar pearls. Finish off with a dusting of sparkling sugar.

8. Let the chocolate cool for 30 minutes, or until it hardens completely. Refrigerate for faster cooling. Be gentle when removing spiderwebs from the parchment paper. Use a spatula if needed.

Mildred Hubble's Hats

MAKES 20 TO 24 WITCH HATS

Indulge in the magical misadventures of Mildred Hubble from *The Worst Witch* with these witch-hat cupcakes. This recipe comes together quickly, contains mostly store-bought ingredients, and are great to make with your own witch-in-training.

SPECIAL EQUIPMENT NEEDED

Stand mixer with paddle attachment, grass piping tip/Ateco 234, icing bag or food-safe plastic bag

INGREDIENTS

1 (15.3 ounces, or 432 g) yellow cake mix (and ingredients to make it according to package directions)

8 to 12 drops green food coloring

16 ounces (454 g) buttercream frosting

8 to 12 drops orange food coloring, or more as needed

½ cup (100 g) powdered sugar

2 boxes (5 ounces, or 142 g) black sugar cones (such as Oreos sugar cones)

1 bag (10 ounces, or 284 g) candy-coated chocolates (such as M&M'S)

1 box (9.75 ounces, or 276 g) mini fudge brownies (24 mini brownies)

3 boxes (8.85 ounces, or 248 g) Dutch cocoa cookies (24 cookies)

· ·

HEED: If you are transporting these anywhere, wait until you are at your destination to place hats on cupcakes.

1. Line a cupcake pan with cupcake liners.

2. Prepare the cake mix according to the package directions, with the addition of green food coloring in the batter. Bake the cupcakes as directed, or until a toothpick inserted into the center comes out clean. Cool the cupcakes in the pan for 10 minutes. Then transfer to a wire rack to completely cool.

3. Empty the frosting into the stand mixer with the paddle attachment. Add the orange food coloring and powdered sugar. (Store-bought frosting tends to be creamy and easily spreadable. Powdered sugar adds stiffness to the frosting so piping details will stay crisp.) Mix until combined. Add extra food coloring as needed to achieve the desired color. Spoon the frosting into the icing bag fitted with the tip and twist closed.

4. Pipe frosting in loops and bows across the tops of the cupcakes. Make sure there are drips along the cupcake edges. The frosting should look like messy, tangled witch hair, so the more mixed up the better. Leave an area of exposed green cupcake to give the appearance of the witch's forehead once the hat is placed on top.

5. To make the witch hats: Prepare the ice cream cones by filling them with candy-coated chocolates. Then place a mini brownie inside each cone and shimmy it down until it snugly fits. This will keep the chocolate candies inside the cone when it is turned over and help the frosting glue the cone and cookie together. Pipe a 2-inch (5-cm) circle of frosting on a cookie and place a stuffed cone on top. Push it down and allow the frosting to create a band around the hat. Add a candy-coated chocolate to the frosting band to look like a buckle or gem detail. Place the completed witch hats directly on top of the cupcakes and press down to secure.

6. Serve and enjoy.

Jack-Be-Littles

MAKES ABOUT 4 DOZEN

Enjoy the flavorful pumpkin cake and tangy cream cheese frosting with these petite treats.

SPECIAL EQUIPMENT NEEDED

Stand mixer with paddle attachment, flour sifter or wire strainer, star piping tip/Ateco 854, icing bag or food-safe plastic bag, Bento food picks, eye-style, 24-cup mini muffin pan

INGREDIENTS

CUPCAKES

¾ cup (90 g) all-purpose flour

½ teaspoon baking powder

½ teaspoon baking soda

¼ teaspoon salt

½ teaspoon ground cinnamon

1 teaspoon pumpkin pie spice

⅔ cup (155 g) pumpkin purée

½ cup (100 g) granulated sugar

½ cup (100 g) brown sugar, packed

3 large eggs

FROSTING

8 ounces (227 g) cream cheese, softened

6 tablespoons (85 g) unsalted butter, room temperature

1 teaspoon vanilla extract

1½ cup (340 g) powdered sugar

Black and orange nonpareils, for dusting

Halloween mix sprinkles, for dusting

1. To make the cupcakes: Preheat the oven to 350°F (175°C, or gas mark 4). Line a mini cupcake tin with paper liners or grease lightly.

2. In a medium-sized bowl, whisk together the flour, baking powder, baking soda, salt, cinnamon, and pumpkin pie spice. Set aside.

3. In the bowl of a stand mixer with a paddle attachment, combine the pumpkin purée, sugar, brown sugar, and eggs.

4. Gradually add the dry ingredients to the wet ingredients. Mix until just combined. Be careful not to overmix, as it can lead to dense cupcakes.

5. Divide the batter evenly among the cupcake tin, filling each liner no more than half full. Bake for 10 to 12 minutes, until a toothpick inserted into the center of a cupcake comes out clean.

6. Remove the cupcakes from the oven and allow them to cool in the pan for 10 minutes before transferring them to a wire rack to cool completely.

7. To make the frosting: In the bowl of a stand mixer with a paddle attachment, beat the softened cream cheese, butter, and vanilla together for 2 minutes, or until smooth and creamy.

8. Using a flour sifter or wire strainer, sift the powdered sugar into the cream cheese mixture. (Sifting removes clumps and helps create light and fluffy frosting). Switch stand mixer to whisk attachment. Mix on low speed until the sugar is just incorporated, scraping down the sides as needed. Increase the speed to high and continue to beat for 1 to 2 minutes, until the frosting is smooth. If piping, spoon the frosting into a piping bag with a tip and twist close. Once the cupcakes have cooled completely, pipe cream cheese frosting in a swirl onto each cupcake.

9. Top with sprinkles and bento food picks.

It Came From the '80s Popcorn Balls

MAKES 8 POPCORN BALLS

This recipe adds crunchy candy and craft sticks into the mix to update this classic 1980s Halloween treat.

SPECIAL EQUIPMENT NEEDED

Candy thermometer (a meat thermometer may be used if it goes up to 392°F, or 200°C, food-grade disposable gloves, craft sticks

INGREDIENTS

½ cup (115 g) unpopped popcorn kernels, or 10 cups (1,250 g) popped popcorn

1 cup (120 g) granulated sugar

1 cup (240 ml) light corn syrup

¼ cup (½ stick or 55 g) unsalted butter

1 teaspoon vanilla extract

½ teaspoon salt

2 or 3 drops food coloring, orange (1 drop red, 2 drops yellow)

Cooking oil spray or ¼ teaspoon vegetable oil

1 box (1.65 ounces, or 46.7 g) sweet crunchy candy (such as Nerds)

½ cup (100 g) candy corn

2 to 3 tablespoons sprinkles

2 to 3 tablespoons candy eyes

1. Pop the popcorn (see page 152 for methods).

2. Line a half baking sheet with parchment paper or a non-slip silicone baking mat.

3. In a large saucepan, combine the sugar, corn syrup, and butter. Place the saucepan over medium heat and stir continuously until the mixture comes to a boil. Insert a thermometer and continue stirring until the mixture reaches 235 to 240°F (113 to 116°C). Remove from the heat.

4. Stir the vanilla extract, salt, and food coloring into the syrup mixture.

5. Pour the syrup mixture over the popped popcorn. Using a wooden spoon or heat-resistant silicone spatula, gently stir the popcorn until it is evenly coated. Be careful because the syrup is very hot.

6. Put on gloves and grease them with cooking oil spray or oil to prevent sticking. Take a handful, about 1 to 1½ cups (230 to 345 g), coated popcorn and press together to form a ball shape. Don't press too firmly or the popcorn will be hard to eat. Roll in the crunchy candy, candy corn, sprinkles, and eye candy. Insert the craft stick about halfway into ball.

7. Lay the popcorn balls on the prepared baking sheet to set. If the mixture becomes too sticky to handle, spray your hands with cooking oil spray again.

8. Let the popcorn balls cool for 30 minutes, or until they are room temperature.

9. Once they have cooled and hardened, the popcorn balls are ready to be enjoyed or wrapped in cellophane bags for up to 5 days.

Banana Split Personality Ice Pops

MAKES 6 ICE POPS

These Banana Split Personality Ice Pops may taste like ice cream, but hidden in plain sight is a delicious dessert made of 100 percent banana. This duality makes for a Jekyll and Hyde–style frozen dessert, in which a seemingly kind and respectable vanilla ice cream has a darker, more sinister alter ego of fruit purée that ultimately leads to its doom. Thankfully, you won't be able to taste the difference! This is a great recipe to make with kids of all ages.

SPECIAL EQUIPMENT NEEDED

6-piece reusable silicone ice pop mold (3.3 ounces, or 94 g) with reusable craft sticks

INGREDIENTS

3 bananas, peeled and sliced

½ cup (120 g) vanilla yogurt

1 cup (190 g) semisweet chocolate chips

2 teaspoons coconut oil

Confetti sprinkles, for topping

Whipped cream, for topping

6 green maraschino cherries or candy pumpkins, for garnish

1. In a blender, purée the bananas and vanilla yogurt until smooth. Pour into the ice pop molds, insert the craft sticks, and freeze for 6 to 8 hours, until firm throughout.

2. Add the chocolate chips and coconut oil to a wide microwaveable bowl. Microwave at 30-second intervals, stirring after each interval, until the chips are just melted and smooth. Be careful not to overheat the chocolate because it can burn easily.

3. Line a half baking sheet with parchment paper or a non-slip silicone baking mat.

4. Remove the ice pops from the mold. If ice pops are resistant in coming out of the mold, pour warm water over them and gently push ice pop out from the bottom.

5. One at a time, take an ice pop and dip at least one-half to two-thirds of it into melted chocolate. Use a spoon to help coat evenly. Let excess chocolate drip off. Then quickly dip the top one-third of the ice pop into sprinkles or spoon the sprinkles on. Place on a baking sheet.

6. Pipe whipped cream onto the ice pops and top with maraschino cherries or candy pumpkins. Serve immediately. Ice pops can be kept in freezer for up to 2 days (top with whipped cream and cherries right before serving).

Bat Attitude Cake Pops

MAKES 36 TO 40 BATS

This colony, or cauldron, of bewitchingly adorable bat cake pops adds a touch of whimsy sure to enchant any occasion.

SPECIAL EQUIPMENT NEEDED

Stand mixer with whisk attachment, size 40/medium cookie scoop, paper lollipop sticks, toothpicks

INGREDIENTS

1 box (15.3 ounces, or 432 g) white cake mix (and ingredients to make according to package directions)

1 family-sized package (48 count, or equivalent) sandwich cookies (such as Oreos), plus more for decoration

1 cup (240 ml) vanilla icing

2 cups (452 g) candy melts, black

½ cup (90 g) mini chocolate chips

Candy eyes

1. Prepare the cake mix and bake in a 9 × 13 inch (23 × 33 cm) cake pan according to the package directions. Let cool completely.

2. Separate 20 chocolate sandwich cookies. Using a butter knife, scrape off each cookie's filling into a small bowl. Place cookie wafers in a sandwich-size plastic bag and gently mash them into crumbs. Set aside.

3. Break the cake into pieces and place in the bowl of a stand mixer. Whisk on low for 1 minute to crumble the cake. Add the icing and stir until well mixed. Add the cookie crumbs and stir until incorporated. Using a spoon, add small bits of cookie cream into the dough. Stir to combine.

4. Line a half baking sheet with parchment paper or a non-slip silicone baking mat.

5. To make cake balls: Spoon 1½ tablespoons or a size 40/medium cookie scoop of cake mixture and roll it into a ball. Place on the baking sheet. Refrigerate for 30 minutes.

6. Prepare black candy melts, in a microwave-safe bowl (see page 146 for how to melt candy melts).

7. Dip one-fourth of a lollipop stick into candy melt and then insert about halfway into a cake ball. Place on the baking sheet and repeat for remaining cake balls. Refrigerate again for about 30 minutes.

8. To create bat wings: Separate another 20 to 25 cookies into halves and discard each cookie's filling. Break each cookie wafer into two.

9. Reheat candy melts.

10. Dip each cake ball entirely into the candy melt. Gently tap off excess and place on the baking sheet. Press cookie halves into opposite sides of the cake pop and hold until firmly set. Using a toothpick, dab on candy melt to adhere candy eyes and two mini chocolate chips as pointy ears. Repeat for all of the cake balls.

Candy Corn Pretzel Hugs

MAKES ABOUT 72 HUGS

In the darkest corners of the kitchen, where salt and sweetness rendezvous, a spellbinding creation known as Pretzel Hugs emerge. Petite pretzel grids, like delicate offering plates, cradle chocolate dollops to create an irresistible flavor and texture combination. The Halloween King of Candy, candy corn, crowns each confection to produce an easy and cute offering for kids and adults alike.

INGREDIENTS

1 bag (16 ounces, or 454 g) square-shaped pretzels (sometimes called Snaps)

1 bag (10.6 ounces, or 300 g) milk chocolate and white creme striped candy (such as Hershey's Hugs)

1 cup (190 g) candy corn

1. Preheat the oven to 300°F (150°C, or gas mark 2) and line a half baking sheet with parchment paper.

2. Line up the pretzels in rows on the prepared baking sheet. If the pretzels are crowded, prepare an additional baking sheet with parchment paper.

3. Place one unwrapped chocolate candy in the middle of each pretzel.

4. Bake for 2 to 4 minutes, until the chocolate looks wet and shiny. (The chocolate should not melt down or change shape!) Do not bake for more than 5 minutes.

5. Remove the baking sheet from the oven. While the pretzels are still on the baking sheet, place a candy corn on top of each chocolate candy. The chocolate will collapse and hold the candy corn once cool.

6. The chocolate candy will remain relatively soft until cooled overnight. Cooling can be sped up by placing the pretzels in the freezer for 15 minutes.

DID YOU KNOW?

Approximately 35 billion pounds (15 billion kg) of candy corn are made in the U.S. each year.

Cinnamon Roll Snakes on a Plate

MAKES 5 SNAKES

Cinnamon is despised by all serpents and is a great way to keep these slithery creatures out of your home and off your connecting flights.

INGREDIENTS

1 can (17.5 ounces, or 496 g) store-bought cinnamon rolls (with icing included, large or grand size preferred)

1 strawberry fruit leather

10 sugar pearl sprinkles in black, purple, or green

DID YOU KNOW?

Most snakes rise up or lift their head and upper body off the ground while keeping their tail anchored to explore their surroundings, search for food, or simply check you out. It is only exotic snake species, particularly venomous ones, that rise up as a warning before striking.

1. Preheat the oven to 350°F (175°C, or gas mark 4).

2. Line a half baking sheet with parchment paper or foil for easy cleanup.

3. Make 5 loosely packed foil balls, each about the size of a golf ball.

4. On the prepared baking sheet, open the can of cinnamon rolls and separate the dough into individual rolls.

5. Unwrap each cinnamon roll and then loosely wind it back up into a spiral, leaving 3 to 4 inches (7.5 to 10 cm) of the dough end unwrapped and straight out.

6. Using your pointer finger and thumb, carefully pinch the sides of the end of the dough to create a triangle-shaped snake head. Place the foil ball next to dough and gently lay the head onto the ball. The neck will drape down the side of the ball to cradle the dough while baking. Repeat with each cinnamon roll, placing each snake 2 to 3 inches (5 to 7.5 cm) apart.

7. Bake 10 to 18 minutes, until puffed up. Watch carefully so that the snakes do not get too brown. Let cool 2 to 4 minutes.

8. Cut ¼ × 2-inch (6 mm × 5-cm) rectangles from fruit leather using kitchen shears. You will need 5.

9. To create a forked tongue: Cut a triangle out of one short end of each rectangle. Using a toothpick, poke a hole for the mouth and insert fruit leather tongue. Poke holes on each side of the snake's head and insert sugar pearls. Use a dab of icing to make them stick.

10. Spread and drizzle the icing included in the can.

Crispy Beast Beings

MAKES 8 BEASTS

I regret to inform you that I've taken the innocent joy of a crisped rice cereal treat and turned it into something ghoulish, maybe even monstrous. Once simple and sweet, these chewy rectangles are now grotesque figures that resemble creatures from the darkest recesses of the mind. Will you resist the temptation of these adorable abominations?

SPECIAL EQUIPMENT NEEDED

Large sauté pan, soup pot, or Dutch oven; craft sticks or wooden skewers

INGREDIENTS

3 tablespoons butter, plus more to grease casserole dish

4 cups (380 g) marshmallows

6 cups (300 g) rice cereal

½ cup (90 g) Halloween confetti sprinkles, plus more for decorating

1 cup (226 g) candy melts, green

1 cup (226 g) candy melts, blue

Candy eyes, small and large

Metallic pearl sprinkles, for decorating

Black sanding sugar, for decorating

Red string licorice, for decorating

1. Line a 9 x13 in (23 x33 cm) casserole dish with parchment paper or grease it with butter.

2. In a large pot, melt the butter over low heat. Add the marshmallows and stir until melted. Turn off the heat. Add the cereal and confetti sprinkles. Stir until well combined. Press the mixture into the prepared casserole dish until even. Let cool completely.

3. Cut the treats into 8 rectangles. Insert a craft stick or skewer into each rectangle.

4. Line a half baking sheet with parchment paper or a non-slip silicone baking mat.

5. Prepare both green and blue candy melts in microwave-safe bowls (see page 146 for how to melt candy melts).

6. Dip the rectangles into the candy melts and place back on baking sheet to set. Decorate with candy eyes, sprinkles, colored sugar, and licorice. Work fast because candy melts cool quickly.

7. Let cool for 1 hour. Remove craft sticks or skewers and serve. You can store for 3 days in an airtight container with wax paper between layers. Or freeze in a freezer bag for up to 6 weeks.

HEED: If you don't plan on gobbling these all up within a day of making them, add ½ cup (120 ml) sweetened condensed milk along with the melted butter. (The condensed milk makes the treats remain soft and gooey for days). Stir well until the mixture begins to boil or you see small bubbles form in the center of the pot. Follow the remaining recipe directions.

The Upside-Down Pumpkin Pie Cake

MAKES 12 SERVINGS

Step into a dark and decaying dimension with this creative dessert inspired by the popular Netflix series *Stranger Things*. Enter a parallel universe where you pour a pumpkin pie into chocolatey cake batter and out comes a neatly separated, layered confection. You may hesitate to go back to the Right-Side-Up when the Upside-Down offers treats like this.

SPECIAL EQUIPMENT NEEDED

9 × 13 in (23 × 33 cm) cake pan, stand mixer with whisk attachment, pastry bag, Ateco 808 plain piping tip (or large smooth-opening piping tip of your choice) or sandwich-size plastic bag

INGREDIENTS

1 box (15.25 ounce) devil's food cake mix (and ingredients to make as stated on box)

1 × 15 oz can (425 g) pumpkin purée

½ cup (120 ml) evaporated milk

1½ cups (360 ml) heavy cream, divided

3 eggs

1 cup (200 g) brown sugar

1½ teaspoons pumpkin pie spice

¼ cup (50 g) powdered sugar

1 teaspoon vanilla extract

2 tablespoons marshmallow cream or 2 to 3 large marshmallows, melted

1 tablespoon black confetti sprinkles

½ cup (115 g) candy pumpkins (such as Mellowcreme)

1. Preheat the oven to 350°F (175°C, or gas mark 4), then grease the cake pan.

2. Prepare the cake mix according to the package instructions and pour into the prepared cake pan. Set aside. (Do not bake, yet!)

3. In a large bowl, whisk together the pumpkin purée, evaporated milk, ½ cup (120 ml) of the heavy cream, eggs, brown sugar, and pumpkin pie spice until smooth.

4. Slowly pour the pumpkin mixture into pan with the cake mix. Carefully place the cake pan into the oven and bake for 50 to 60 minutes or until you can insert a toothpick into the middle and it comes out clean. Cool to room temperature.

5. In the bowl of a stand mixer fitted with the whisk attachment, beat the remaining 1 cup (240 ml) heavy cream, powdered sugar, and vanilla extract. Stop the beater and add the marshmallow cream or melted marshmallows to the whipped cream, and continue whipping on high until stiff peaks form.

6. If piping, spoon the whipped cream into a icing bag with a tip or sandwich-size plastic bag with bottom corner cut off. Begin piping the whipped cream in a swirl and release as you pull up to form a soft top.

7. Place black confetti sprinkles for eyes and howling mouths. Set candy pumpkins next to ghosts or place throughout.

8. Serve immediately, or chill until ready to eat. Either way it tastes great. Enjoy!

Spell Book S'mores

MAKES 6 SPELL BOOKS

A Spell Book S'more is a magical twist on the classic campfire treat. It features graham crackers, melted chocolate, and a marshmallow filling infused with the witchy wisdom of once-resourceful and capable folk-healing women.

SPECIAL EQUIPMENT NEEDED

Craft sticks

INGREDIENTS

6 graham crackers, full rectangles

½ cup (120 ml) marshmallow fluff

1½ cupsw (190 g) semi-sweet chocolate chips

1 cup (226 g) green candy melts

Candy eyes, for topping

Metallic pearl sprinkles, for topping

. . . .

HEED: Make fluffernutter Spell Book S'mores! After spreading marshmallow fluff, spread 1 tablespoon of peanut butter on each graham cracker. Continue with recipe directions.

1. Break each graham cracker into 2 squares, for a total of 12 squares. Spread about 1 tablespoon of marshmallow fluff on each of the 6 squares. Place the top third of a craft stick on top of each. Place the remaining 6 graham cracker squares on top and press down to make sandwiches. (Craft sticks make it easy to handle graham cracker sandwiches while dipping them in chocolate and decorating.)

2. Freeze each sandwich for about 20 minutes, or until the marshmallow fluff is firm.

3. Line a half baking sheet with parchment paper or a non-slip silicone baking mat.

4. Add the chocolate chips to a wide, deep microwaveable bowl. Cook at 30-second intervals, stirring after each interval, until the chocolate is just melted and smooth. Be careful not to overheat the chocolate because it can burn easily.

5. Remove the sandwiches from the freezer. Hold each sandwich by the craft stick and dip it into the melted chocolate. Use a spoon to help coat the entire sandwich evenly. Let excess chocolate drip off and place back onto the prepared baking sheet.

6. Freeze the sandwiches for about 20 minutes, or until the chocolate has solidified.

7. Prepare the green candy melts in a microwave-safe, sandwich-size plastic bag (see page 146 for how to melt candy melts).

8. Cut a tiny tip from the bottom corner of the plastic bag and decorate each spell book with spider webs, all-knowing eyes, spirals, and whatever other chilling details tickle your fancy. Make sure to pipe book cover hinges and raised bands along the sandwich edge to make it look like a book! Top with candy eyes and sprinkles.

Creepmas

Creepmas is an eerie, unsettling celebration of Christmas. Blending elements of Halloween magic, goth aesthetics, and dark humor, these recipes offer an absurd and entertaining way to embrace that other holiday season. Have some fun and trade the traditional red and green for black Christmas trees, twinkling purple lights, and silver skeleton Santas. Imagine a menu featuring salads that bite back, presents wrapped in bacon, and cookies for the beast who comes for those on the naughty list. Make this yuletide a time to savor the unusual and elevate the off-kilter. Season's Creepings!

Man-Eating Wreath Salad

MAKES 1 LARGE WREATH (2 ENTREES OR 4 SIDES)

In *Disney Tim Burton's The Nightmare Before Christmas* (1993), a man-eating plant disguised as a wreath wreaks havoc by sprouting tentacles and gobbling up a holiday reveler. Now disguised as an Italian house salad with a tangy shallot vinaigrette, this holiday wreath will put your taste buds on alert . . . and make you second-guess the holiday decor on your front door.

SPECIAL EQUIPMENT NEEDED
Immersion blender

INGREDIENTS
VINAIGRETTE

2 tablespoons red wine vinegar

2 tablespoons minced shallot

1 teaspoon Dijon mustard

¼ teaspoon kosher salt

Dash ground black pepper, or to taste

6 tablespoons extra-virgin olive oil

SALAD

1 head romaine lettuce, chopped into bite-size pieces

1 English cucumber, peeled and chopped

2 ribs celery, chopped

¼ small red onion, thinly sliced into half-moons

4 ounces (118 g, or 2 slices) sharp provolone, thinly sliced and cut

2 pepperoncini peppers, whole

1 olive, pitted and cut in half

¼ pound (113 g, or 4 thin slices) salami lunch meat

1. To make the vinaigrette: Combine the red wine vinegar, shallot, mustard, salt, and pepper in a liquid measuring cup and stir well. Blend using an immersion blender, slowly drizzling in the olive oil. (The gradual addition of oil helps emulsify the dressing, creating a smooth and creamy texture.) Keep blending until the oil is fully incorporated. Taste and adjust the seasonings as needed. You'll have about ¾ cup (180 ml) vinaigrette.

2. To make the salad: Combine the lettuce, cucumber, celery, and sliced red onion in a large bowl. Add ⅓ cup (75 ml) vinaigrette and toss well. Taste and add additional vinaigrette if needed.

3. On a serving plate, assemble the wreath by arranging the chopped salad in an 11-inch (28-cm) circle with a large hole in the middle. Place cheese triangles as teeth along the interior of the circle. Arrange pepperoncini peppers as eyes and place olive pupils on top.

4. To make the loops for the salami bow: Fold one salami slice in half, and fold it in half again. Repeat to create both sides of the bow. For bow tails, fold one salami slice in thirds and, using kitchen shears, cut the end at an angle. Place under one loop. Repeat for the other tail. For the bow center, fold the salami trimmed from the tails into thirds and then fold in half. Place between the loops.

DID YOU KNOW?

Jack's presents to the children include nods to past Tim Burton films. The black and white snake resembles a sandworm, and the shrunken head appears in the afterlife waiting room from *Beetlejuice* (1988). Both the cat and duck toys allude to *Batman Returns* (1992).

Belsnickel's Feetloaf

MAKES 4 TO 6 SERVINGS

This chilling take on traditional meatloaf celebrates Belsnickel, a menacing fur-clad and antlered figure of German and Pennsylvania Dutch Christmas traditions. After tapping on your window, he'll burst into your home to either reward you with small toys or cakes or punish you with a swift whipping. Like Belsnickel, this macabre, foot-shaped creation is guaranteed to be the spine-tingling centerpiece of your Creepmas table.

SPECIAL EQUIPMENT NEEDED
Food-grade disposable gloves, pastry brush

INGREDIENTS
SAUCE

¼ cup (60 ml) ketchup

¼ cup (60 ml) barbeque sauce

2 tablespoons (28 g) brown sugar

BEEF

Cooking oil spray

1½ pounds (680 g) lean ground beef

½ teaspoon salt

¼ teaspoon ground black pepper

½ cup (60 g) breadcrumbs

½ cup (50 g) rolled oats

½ cup (60 g) onion, finely chopped

½ cup (90 g) red bell pepper, finely chopped

½ cup (90 g) green bell pepper, finely chopped

½ cup (58 g) shredded Cheddar cheese

¼ cup (60 ml) ketchup

½ cup (120 ml) milk

1 onion layer

2 celery ribs (optional)

1. To make the sauce: Stir together the ketchup, barbeque sauce, and brown sugar in a small bowl. Set aside.

2. To cook the beef: Preheat the oven to 350°F (175°C, or gas mark 4). Prepare a baking sheet lined with aluminum foil and coat with cooking oil spray.

3. In a large mixing bowl, mix the beef, salt, pepper, breadcrumbs, oats, onion, peppers, cheese, ketchup, and milk until well combined.

4. Put on gloves and empty the meat mixture onto a baking sheet. Mold and shape the mixture to resemble a foot. To make the base of the foot: Use your hands and fingers to shape the beef mixture into a rough oval or rectangular form. Use a knife to carve out toe shapes at one end of the oval. Then sculpt the mixture into the general shape of a foot, paying attention to the arch, heel, and ball. It may take some time and patience to get the desired shape. Using kitchen shears, cut 5 toenail shapes, from big toe to pinky toe, from the onion layer. Position the onion toenails appropriately on foot loaf.

5. With a pastry brush, paint the sauce on the foot to add flavor and give it a darker, more menacing appearance.

6. Bake the foot for 45 to 60 minutes, or until its internal temperature reaches 160°F (71°C).

7. Carefully remove the foot from the oven and let it rest for 10 minutes. Insert optional celery ribs into the heel/ankle side of foot to mimic broken leg bones for an extra gruesome detail. Arrange on a platter and enjoy a very Creepmas meal.

Wicked Winter Poultry with Blood Orange Glaze

MAKES 2 TO 4 SERVINGS

In a dimly lit Creepmas gathering, friends gather to celebrate the sinister side of holiday traditions with an unconventional feast. The table, adorned with shadowy ephemera and crimson accents, sets the stage for a phantasmagoric twist on a conventional holiday favorite: a succulent turkey breast, drenched in a crimson glaze, that rests on a bed of blood oranges and aromatic rosemary.

SPECIAL EQUIPMENT NEEDED
Dutch oven

INGREDIENTS

GLAZE

4 blood oranges, squeezed to make about ½ to ¾ cup (120 to 180 ml) juice (See Heed)

½ cup (120 ml) maple syrup

2 tablespoons soy sauce

2 cloves garlic, minced

¼ teaspoon ground cloves

½ teaspoon ground allspice

1 teaspoon paprika

TURKEY

1 (3 pound, or 1.4 kg) boneless turkey breast

3 tablespoons olive oil

1 teaspoon garlic powder

1 teaspoon salt

1 teaspoon ground black pepper

1 blood orange, sliced into thin rounds, for garnish

Fresh rosemary sprigs, for garnish

1. Preheat the oven to 350°F (175°C, or gas mark 4).

2. To prepare the glaze: Combine the orange juice, maple syrup, soy sauce, garlic, cloves, allspice, and paprika in a medium saucepan. Simmer the mixture over low heat until it thickens and forms a glaze, 10 to 15 minutes. Set aside.

3. Rub the turkey with olive oil and season generously with garlic powder, salt, and pepper.

4. Place the seasoned turkey in a Dutch oven or roasting pan.

5. Roast the turkey for 45 to 90 minutes, basting with glaze every 20 to 30 minutes. (Follow the roasting instructions on the turkey breast packaging if available.) Turkey should reach an internal temperature of 165°F (74°C) in the thickest part of the meat.

6. Let rest for about 10 minutes before carving.

7. Arrange the orange rounds and rosemary sprigs on a serving platter. Carve the turkey and arrange slices on the serving platter. The deep red color of the blood oranges will add to the Creepmas aesthetic.

HEED: Don't have access to blood oranges? Use juicing oranges or orange juice instead and add 1 to 2 drops of red food coloring to create a comparable taste and effect.

Roasted Nightshades

MAKES 4 SERVINGS

Some of the earliest-known cultivation of nightshade plants happened around 7000 BCE in what is now Mexico and Peru. Once linked to witchcraft and magic, nightshades have been believed to possess powers related to love, beauty, and protection against evil. Their association with shape-shifting and death prediction added to their mystique. Today, science tells us non-poisonous nightshades are incredibly healthy—full of antioxidants and high in fiber—so this recipe may or may not have more benefits than just what meets the eye.

INGREDIENTS

1 pound (454 g) mini red potatoes, chopped into 1-inch (3-cm) cubes

3 tablespoons olive oil, divided

1 medium eggplant, chopped into 1-inch (3-cm) cubes

3 bell peppers, red, orange, and yellow, cored, de-seeded, and chopped into 1-inch (3-cm) cubes

10 ounces (283 g) grape tomatoes

5 cloves garlic, peeled and thinly sliced

½ teaspoon salt

¼ teaspoon ground black pepper

1 to 2 teaspoons fresh thyme, or ½ teaspoon dried thyme

HEED: Roasted nightshades can be enjoyed as a side dish, tossed into salads, used as pizza toppings, or incorporated into other recipes.

1. Preheat the oven to 425°F (220°C, or gas mark 7). Prepare a half baking sheet with foil for easy cleanup.

2. Place the potatoes on the baking sheet and drizzle with 1 tablespoon of olive oil, ensuring all the vegetables are lightly coated. Roast the potatoes for 20 minutes.

3. While the potatoes are roasting, combine the eggplant, bell peppers, grape tomatoes, garlic, salt, pepper, and thyme with the remaining 2 tablespoons olive oil in a large bowl.

4. Remove the potatoes from the oven and add the vegetable mixture. Spread the vegetables in a single layer on the baking sheet, careful not to overcrowd.

5. Roast for 20 minutes. Gently stir. Roast for another 20 minutes, or until the vegetables are fork-tender and slightly caramelized. The exact roasting time may vary.

6. Serve warm and enjoy!

DID YOU KNOW?

Members of the plant family *Solanaceae* include thousands of species, many of which are nightshades. Like most families, *Solanaceae* has members that are healthy and high in fiber (such as tomatoes, peppers, eggplants, and potatoes) as well as members who are poisonous and inedible (such as tobacco, belladonna, and mandrake.)

Pork Chop Presents

MAKES 4 PRESENTS

Pork chops, bacon-wrapped like gifts, deliver a savory yuletide treat. Bacon's saltiness complements pork's sweetness, creating a flavorful festive offering for your palate.

INGREDIENTS

½ teaspoon dried thyme

½ teaspoon garlic powder

1 teaspoon salt

½ teaspoon ground black pepper

1¼ pounds (567 g) pork ribeye chops boneless (about 4 chops)

1 pound (454 g) hickory smoked bacon (16 bacon slices needed)

1. Prepare two half baking sheets with foil; one for pork chops and one for bacon.

2. In a small bowl, stir the thyme, garlic powder, salt, and pepper. Pat the pork chops dry with paper towels. Rub this seasoning onto both sides of the meat. Let marinate for 30 to 45 minutes.

3. To prepare and cook 4 bacon bows: Preheat the oven to 400°F (205°C, or gas mark 6). You will need 8 slices of bacon and 8 foil cylinders (see page 149 for how to create foil cylinders). On a baking sheet, make a plus sign (+) using 2 pieces of bacon.

4. To create bow loops: Fold the ends of the horizontal bacon slice into the center. Place foil cylinders inside each loop so the bacon slice is supported. Fold the top of the vertical bacon slice down over the center, loosely tuck it under, and bring it back over the top and down to form a knot. Use toothpicks to keep the bacon in place and prevent curling while cooking. Cook for 10 to 25 minutes, until crisp and deep brown. While the bacon is still warm, gently wiggle it out of the foil. Move the bows to paper towels to catch grease. If the bacon tears, use a toothpick to pin it back into place until cool.

5. Wrap each pork chop in bacon, using 2 bacon slices: lay first bacon slice horizontally on pork chop and tuck ends under. Lay second bacon slice on pork chop, perpendicular to first slice, and tuck ends. Secure with toothpicks to prevent curling.

6. Place the pork chops on the prepared baking sheet. Bake for 15 to 20 minutes, until the internal temperature reaches 140°F (63°C). Flip halfway through. Cooking time may vary depending on the thickness of the pork chops, so use a meat thermometer. Then broil on high for 2 minutes to crisp the bacon. Remove the pork chops from the oven and let them rest for 5 minutes.

7. Delicately arrange the bacon bows on top of the pork chops and serve.

O Creepmas Tree

MAKES 1 TREE, SERVES 7 TO 10

A unique and visually striking twist on a tried-and-true holiday symbol.

SPECIAL EQUIPMENT NEEDED

Mini bat cookie cutter,
pastry brush

INGREDIENTS

1 package puff pastry sheets with
two sheets in box

1 to 2 tablespoons all-purpose
flour, for dusting work surface

¾ cup (177 ml) poppy seed cake
and pastry filling

1 egg, beaten, for egg wash

1 teaspoon heavy cream or milk
of choice, for egg wash

2 tablespoons coarse white
sugar

2 tablespoons honey

HEED: Some puff pastry brands
require 6 to 8 hours or overnight
refrigeration to thaw. Plan
accordingly!

1. Preheat the oven to 400°F (205°C, or gas mark 6) and line a half baking sheet with parchment paper or a non-slip silicone baking mat.

2. Dust a baking sheet with 1 tablespoon flour and unfold one sheet of the pastry on top. If the pastry cracks while unfolding, wet fingers and press the edges of the crack together.

3. Spread an even layer of poppy seed filling across the entire pastry, leaving a slight border around the edges. Place a second sheet of pastry on top of the first sheet and carefully unroll.

4. With a knife, gently make small marks every 1 inch (2.5 cm) to 1½ inches (4 cm) alongside the left and right edges of the pastry. Find the middle of the pastry sheet and make a faint line all the way down.

5. With a pizza cutter or kitchen shears and using marks as a guide, cut horizontal strips of pastry to about ½-inch (1.3 cm) from the center mark. Do not cut all the way across. Repeat on the other side. Gently twist each strip 3 or 4 times.

6. Cut the pastry into a triangle shape by slicing from the top center of the pastry to the lower outside edges. Set aside the excess pastry.

7. With the excess pastry bits, make a star by placing 5 small pieces in a circle and pinching together at the center. Combine the remaining pastry and roll out until ¼ inch (6 mm) thick. Cut out bats with the cookie cutter. Attach all to the tree with the filling.

8. In a small bowl, whisk together the egg and heavy cream. Brush the egg wash over the entire tree. Then sprinkle with coarse sugar. Bake for 15 to 20 minutes, until golden. Let cool for 5 minutes.

9. Carefully transfer the pastry to a serving platter. Cut between each twist if they are stuck together. Drizzle with honey and enjoy!

Krampus Kookies

Krampus Kookies are a festive treat for those who misbehave this holiday season. These cookies come together easily with a store-bought mix, so time can be spent on decorating. Add-ins of lemon zest and vanilla elevate their taste, while the fanciful Krampus candy melt silhouette and crushed peppermint candy bring on the holiday fear . . . I mean cheer.

SPECIAL EQUIPMENT NEEDED

Size 40 cookie scoop, Flat Krampus or goat head silhouette about 2 inches (5 cm) in diameter

INGREDIENTS

1 pouch (6.3 ounces, or 177 g) Sugar Cookie Mix (and ingredients to make it according to package directions)

1 tablespoon lemon zest (zest of approximately 1 lemon)

1 teaspoon vanilla extract

1 cup (170 g) candy melts, red

¼ cup (50 g) candy cane or peppermint candy, crushed (optional)

DID YOU KNOW?

A creature from European folklore, Krampus is a terrifying half-goat, half-demon that visits naughty children every year on Krampusnact in December.

1. Preheat the oven to the temperature stated on the cookie mix packaging. Prepare a half baking sheet with parchment paper or a non-slip silicone baking mat.

2. In a large bowl, prepare the cookie mix. To enhance flavor, stir in the lemon zest and vanilla.

3. Roll 1 size 40 cookie scoop, or 2 tablespoons of dough into a ball and place it on the prepared baking sheet. Repeat with the remaining dough, leaving about 2 inches (5 cm) of space between cookies.

4. Bake for the amount of time stated on the cookie mix package, or until the cookie edges are lightly golden and the centers are slightly cracked. Cookie centers may appear slightly soft, but they will firm up as they cool.

5. Let cool 1 minute. Gently press the cookies flat with a spatula. Place the Krampus silhouette on each flat cookie and press down to make an indentation. Remove the silhouette from the cookie. The goal is an imprint, so do not press all the way down.

6. Let the cookies cool on the baking sheet for 5 minutes. Transfer to a wire rack to cool completely, about 30 minutes.

7. Prepare red candy melts in a microwave-safe, sandwich-size plastic bag (see page 146 for how to melt candy melts).

8. Cut a tiny tip from the bottom corner of the plastic bag and squeeze candy melt into the Krampus imprints. Jiggle each cookie from side to side to evenly distribute. Be careful not to overfill. Sprinkle with crushed peppermint candy, if preferred.

9. Let rest for 20 to 30 minutes for the candy melts to harden.

Annabelle Pastries

MAKES 8 PASTRIES

This thrilling, chilling version of a classic toaster pastry is greatly simplified by using store-bought pie crusts and a filling that comes together quickly.

SPECIAL EQUIPMENT NEEDED

4-inch (10-cm) gingerbread cookie cutter, pastry brush

INGREDIENTS

DOUGH

1 box (14.01 oz) refrigerated pie crusts (2 crusts per box)

¼ cup (30 g) all-purpose flour, for dusting work surface

FILLING

¼ cup (50 g) brown sugar

1 tablespoon unsalted butter, melted

¼ teaspoon ground cinnamon

¼ teaspoon vanilla extract

Dash salt

1 egg, for egg wash

1 tablespoon half-and-half, or milk of choice, for egg wash

GLAZE

2 teaspoons half-and-half or milk of choice

½ cup (100 g) powdered sugar

¼ teaspoon maple flavoring

1. To prepare the dough: Follow the pie crust package directions to bring the crust dough to room temperature. Preheat the oven to 400°F (205°C, or gas mark 6) and line a half baking sheet with parchment paper or a non-slip silicone baking mat.

2. To make the filling: Mix the sugar, butter, cinnamon, vanilla, and salt until crumbly in a medium bowl.

3. To make the pastries: Unroll one pie crust onto a flour-dusted surface. Do this slowly and delicately to prevent cracks. Cut 8 bodies out of dough with the cookie cutter. If the cookie cutter does not easily release from the dough, dip into flour before cutting. Carefully place each body on the prepared baking sheet, spaced about 1 to 2 inches (2.5 to 5 cm) apart. Spoon ¼ to ½ teaspoon brown sugar mixture onto the dough, sprinkling evenly throughout. Make sure to leave a ⅛- to ¼-inch (3 to 6 mm) clean edge around each body.

4. Unroll the second pie crust onto the floured surface and cut out 8 more bodies. Using a toothpick, poke details into each dough body: eyes, nose, mouth, buttons, bracelets, anklets, and so on. These holes allow steam to escape and prevent the pastries from exploding while baking.

5. With water, lightly moisten the edges around each dough body on the baking sheet. Place a second dough body on top of each moistened one. Use a fork to firmly crimp and seal the edges together to prevent the filling from leaking during baking.

6. Crack the egg into a small bowl and whisk in 1 tablespoon half-and-half or milk. Using a pastry brush, brush egg wash onto the surface of each body.

7. Bake for 12 to 15 minutes, until golden brown. Let cool for 15 to 20 minutes.

8. Meanwhile, make the glaze: Combine the milk, powdered sugar, and maple flavoring in a small bowl and mix well. Spoon the glaze into a plastic sandwich bag and cut a tiny tip from one of the bottom corners to make a piping bag. Twist the bag from above to close and push the glaze down in to the corner. Continue twisting and squeezing to pipe the glaze on the bodies. Be creative with hair bows, aloof eyebrows, complicated smiles, lacy frills, and empty hearts.

9. Serve when the glaze has hardened.

Baba Yaga's Butternut Squash and Sage Brown Butter Pasta

MAKES 2-4 SERVINGS

This warm, comforting dish combines the earthy sweetness of caramelized butternut squash with the nutty richness of browned butter, aromatic sage, and tangy Parmesan. It's something Baba Yaga could really sink her iron teeth into.

SPECIAL EQUIPMENT NEEDED

Large skillet or fry pan, large bowl

INGREDIENTS

2 tablespoons olive oil

1 medium-sized butternut squash, peeled, de-seeded, and cut into cubes (about 4 to 5 cups, or 360 to 700 g; see page 151 for how to peel a butternut squash)

8 ounces (225 g) pasta mini farfalle

1 to 2 teaspoons salt

4 tablespoons unsalted butter

⅓ cup (40 g) shallots, sliced

12 to 15 fresh sage leaves

1 teaspoon lemon juice

½ cup (80 g) shredded Parmesan cheese, plus more for serving

Salt and ground black pepper, to taste

1. In a large skillet over medium-high heat, add the olive oil. Once hot, add the squash and stir to coat. Sauté for 8 to 15 minutes, until softened and caramelized. Remove from heat and set aside. .

2. In a large pot, salt some water and cook pasta to al dente according to package directions. Drain and set aside, reserving about 2 cups (480 ml) of pasta water.

3. While the pasta is cooking, melt the butter over medium heat in the skillet. Cook for 5 to 8 minutes. It will foam and then change to a golden tan.

4. As soon as it changes color, add the shallots, sage leaves, and lemon juice. Cook for 1 to 2 minutes, until the leaves become crispy. Remove from heat. Carefully remove the sage leaves and set them aside for garnish.

5. Return the squash to the skillet and stir gently to coat with browned butter. Add the cooked pasta and 1 cup (240 ml) reserved pasta water. Return to the burner and decrease the heat to medium. Stir until the pasta, squash, and brown butter are well combined. Simmer until the pasta is fully cooked, 2 to 3 minutes. Add additional pasta water to prevent sticking and increase sauciness, ½ cup (120 ml) at a time.

6. Remove from the heat. Toss in the Parmesan and season with salt and pepper to taste.

7. Top with crispy sage leaves and additional Parmesan.

Haunted House Mouse Cookies

MAKES 24 COOKIES

The Little Mouse, or La Petite Souris, is a character from French folklore who collects lost teeth and leaves a small gift in exchange. In some modern versions, the Little Mouse takes pleasure in stealing the teeth of little children. Playful or frightening? Something to ponder as you munch on these tasty cookies.

SPECIAL EQUIPMENT NEEDED

Food processor, rubber spatula, size 40 cookie scoop, wooden skewer

INGREDIENTS

1 cup (120 g) slivered almonds

2 to 3 cups (240 g to 360 g) powdered sugar, divided

1 cup (230 g) unsalted butter, sliced and room temperature

1 teaspoon vanilla extract

¼ teaspoon salt

2 cups (250 g) all-purpose flour, plus more for dusting parchment paper

12 cherry or red pieces pull-apart licorice, separated and cut in half

Tube of red gel icing, to decorate

HEED: Like mice, these cookies can cause a mess. Most, but not all, of the powdered sugar will stick to the mouse once it has completely cooled.

1. In a food processor, pulse the almonds and 1 cup (120 g) powdered sugar until sand-like crumbs form.

2. Add the butter and vanilla. Process until smooth, 1 to 2 minutes at most. Scrape down the side of the bowl as needed. Add the salt and flour and pulse. Again, scrape down the sides as needed. When thoroughly combined, the dough will be wet and sticky.

3. Using a rubber spatula, turn the dough out onto flour-dusted parchment paper and shape into a 14 to 15-inch (36 to 38-cm) log. Refrigerate for 20 to 30 minutes.

4. Preheat the oven to 350°F (175°C, or gas mark 4). Line 2 cookie sheets with parchment paper or non-slip silicone baking mats to prevent sticking.

5. Make a ball with about 2 tablespoons or a cookie scoop of dough. Using your hands, roll or pinch the dough into a slight point to create a mouse shape. If the dough is sticky while rolling, dust your hands with powdered sugar.

6. Place the dough on the prepared baking sheet. The cookies will spread and flatten while baking, so place them at least 2 inches (5 cm) apart. Bake for 15 to 18 minutes, until the bottoms of the cookies are light brown.

7. Cool for 5 minutes. While still warm, dredge each cookie entirely in the remaining powdered sugar and place on a cooling rack. Insert 2 slivered almonds on each head to create ears. Using a wooden skewer, poke a deep hole in each tail end and insert the licorice. (Because of the size of the licorice tail, use a wooden skewer instead of a toothpick.)

8. Let cool completely. Create eyes and nose with small dots of red gel icing. Serve.

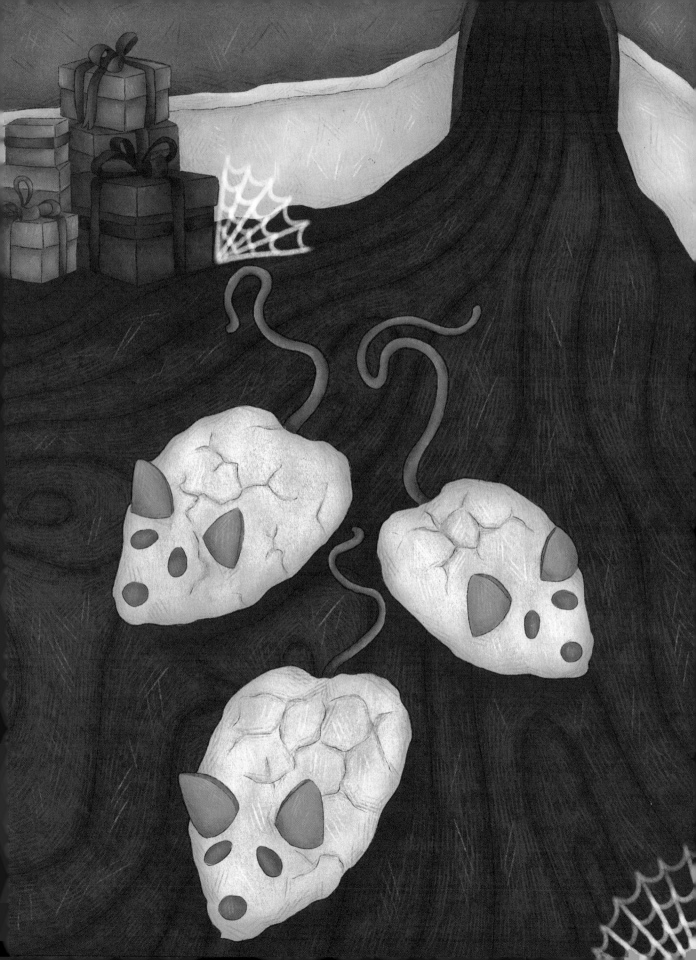

#
Goth Valentine's Day

Welcome to the mysterious realm of Goth Valentine's Day. It's a holiday traditionally soaked in sweet messages and colorful hearts. This unconventional take on Valentine's Day honors the tortured souls that yearn for a love beyond the ordinary. This is a day where black roses bloom, delicate lace veils the daylight, and candles flicker in shadowy corners. It's a melancholic opportunity for a bittersweet meal of deep dark chocolate, smoky spices, and sometimes acerbic flavors. What follows is a bewitching feast that serves up a symphony of cryptic passion for you and your most sinister sweetheart.

Hester Prynne's bAked Oatmeal

MAKES 4 SERVINGS

Hester Prynne, from Nathaniel Hawthorne's *The Scarlet Letter*, is one of the most tortured, romantic anti-heroes ever to have loved and lost. Pantry staples come together ahead of time so you can wake up and face another day with this deliciously warm, sweetly spiced meal for breakfast or brunch. Enjoy this alone, with your child, or with your favorite unmarried secret sinner.

INGREDIENTS

1 to 2 teaspoons vegetable oil, or cooking oil spray

2 cups (200 g) old-fashioned rolled oats

1 teaspoon baking powder

1 teaspoon ground cinnamon

¼ teaspoon grated nutmeg

½ teaspoon salt

⅓ cup (75 ml) maple syrup

1½ cups (360 ml) milk, dairy or non-dairy

2 eggs

3 tablespoons melted butter

1 teaspoon vanilla extract

2 cups (380 g) frozen blueberries, divided, plus more for topping

LEMON GLAZE

½ cup (50 g) powdered sugar

1 to 2 teaspoons fresh lemon juice, plus more if needed

1 teaspoon lemon zest

Pinch salt

Yogurt, for serving (optional)

Splash milk, for serving (optional)

1. Grease an 8 × 8 (20 × 20 cm) baking dish or a similar-sized oven-safe dish with vegetable oil or cooking oil spray.

2. In a large mixing bowl, combine the oats, baking powder, cinnamon, nutmeg, and salt.

3. In a medium bowl, whisk the maple syrup, milk, eggs, melted butter, and vanilla.

4. Pour the wet mixture into the dry ingredients and stir well.

5. Place 1½ cups (285 g) of blueberries into the prepared baking dish. Pour the oatmeal mixture over the blueberries, spreading it out evenly. Cover with plastic wrap and refrigerate for 8 hours or overnight.

6. Preheat the oven to 350°F (175°C, gas mark 4).

7. Remove the oatmeal from the refrigerator and remove the plastic wrap. Scatter the remaining ½ cup (95 g) blueberries on top, or arrange them into a capital letter A.

8. Bake for 30 to 45 minutes on the middle rack, until the oatmeal is set and the top is golden brown. Let cool for 5 to 10 minutes.

9. To make the glaze: Sift the powdered sugar into a medium bowl to remove any lumps. While whisking, gradually add the lemon juice, lemon zest, and a pinch of salt to the powdered sugar. Whisk until the powdered sugar is fully dissolved and the glaze is smooth. The glaze should be thick but pourable. (To thin, add more lemon juice or water; to thicken, add more powdered sugar.) Drizzle over the cooled oatmeal.

10. Serve the oatmeal on its own or with a side of remaining glaze, a dollop of yogurt, or a splash of milk.

Rip Out My Heart Pull-Apart Bread

MAKES 6 TO 8 SERVINGS

This garlic and cheese pull-apart bread is a great appetizer or side dish for sharing with that special someone.

INGREDIENTS

1 tablespoon vegetable oil, or cooking oil spray

1 can (16.3 ounces, or 453 g) refrigerated biscuit dough

1 cup (120 g) shredded mozzarella cheese

¼ cup (56 g) shredded Cheddar cheese

¼ cup (56 g) shredded Parmesan cheese

6 tablespoons (¾ stick or 85 g) unsalted butter, melted

½ teaspoon garlic powder, or 2 or 3 cloves fresh garlic, minced

1½ teaspoons Italian seasoning

1 tablespoon fresh flat-leaf parsley, chopped

1. Preheat the oven according to the instructions on the biscuit can, usually around 375°F (190°C, or gas mark 5). Generously grease a 9 × 13 inch (23 × 33 cm) casserole dish with oil or cooking oil spray.

2. Open the biscuit dough and separate into individual biscuits. Cut each biscuit into quarters and roll the quarters into balls.

3. In a medium shallow bowl, combine the mozzarella cheese, Cheddar cheese, and Parmesan.

4. In a small bowl, stir together the melted butter, garlic, and Italian seasoning.

5. Dip each dough ball into the garlic butter mixture. Set aside any extra. Then roll in the shredded cheeses, making sure it is thoroughly covered.

6. Place the cheese-coated dough balls into casserole dish in the shape of a heart: Start by arranging two dough balls at the top center of the baking dish, slightly touching. Then place a row of dough balls above the center two, forming the upper curve of the heart. Extend two lines of dough balls outward and downward from the center, forming the lower curves of the heart. Place balls on top of the first layer and adjust as needed. Do not crowd; the dough balls will expand while baking. Top with any remaining cheese mixture.

7. Bake according to the biscuit can instructions, or until the heart is golden brown and the cheese is bubbly, 15 to 20 minutes.

8. Let cool for 3 to 5 minutes. Gently transfer the heart to a serving dish, brush with any reserved butter, and sprinkle with chopped fresh parsley for added flavor and color.

9. Rip apart and enjoy!

Forget-Me-Not Beet Salad

MAKES 4 SIDE SALADS OR 2 DINNER SALADS

Why put your heart on your sleeve when you can serve it up on a plate? Create this truly unique salad for your love to remember you always. The deep-red beet hearts are visually stunning, and their taste is slightly sweet, with just a hint of bitterness. This is the perfect dish with which to remember difficult love stories, relationships that didn't make it, and missed connections.

SPECIAL EQUIPMENT NEEDED

Mini heart cookie cutter

SALAD

2–3 medium-sized beets, scrubbed clean or 1 (8 ounces, or 227 g) package ready-to-eat beets

1 bag (7 ounces, or 198 g) pre-washed arugula (or rocket) leaves

1 large navel orange, supremed (see page 149 instructions)

¼ small red onion, thinly sliced

2 ounces (55 g) crumbled goat cheese

¼ cup (40 g) sea-salted mixed vegetable chips (optional)

VINAIGRETTE DRESSING

3 tablespoons orange juice

1 tablespoon balsamic vinegar

¼ cup (60 ml) extra-virgin olive oil

1 tablespoon honey

¼ teaspoon salt

⅛ teaspoon ground black pepper

1. To make the salad: Preheat the oven to 400°F (205°C, or gas mark 6). Line a half baking sheet with foil.

2. If using raw beets, trim off the tops and bottoms and individually wrap them with foil. Place the wrapped beets on a baking sheet in case any beet juice leaks out. Roast for about 1 hour, or until they are easily pierced with a fork. Once they are cool enough to touch, unwrap the foil and remove the beet skins. If using ready-to-eat beets, skip this step.

3. While the beets are cooking, make the vinaigrette: In a small bowl, combine the orange juice, balsamic vinegar, olive oil, honey, salt, and pepper and mix well. Taste and adjust seasoning to your liking.

4. Cut the beets into ¼-inch (6-mm) slices. Using the cookie cutter, cut heart shapes from the beet slices.

5. Toss the arugula with 2 to 3 tablespoons of vinaigrette. Arrange on plates.

6. Compose individual salads with beet hearts, supremed orange slices, red onion, goat cheese, and vegetable chips. Drizzle with additional vinaigrette, if desired.

HEED: Beets will stain your hands, clothes, and anything they touch. Unless you are Lady Macbeth symbolically trying to wash away the metaphorical bloodstains of your misdeeds, wear gloves and use caution!

Black Velvet Whoopie Pies

MAKES 10 WHOOPIE PIES

This sinfully bewitching black chocolate and pink strawberry dessert will enchant your taste buds and delight your goth aesthetic.

SPECIAL EQUIPMENT NEEDED

Stand mixer with paddle and whisk attachments, ice cream scoop

INGREDIENTS

2 cups (250 g) all-purpose flour

¾ cup (95 g) unsweetened black cocoa powder

1 teaspoon baking soda

¼ teaspoon salt

½ cup (1 stick or 115 g) unsalted butter, room temperature

½ cup (100 g) granulated sugar

½ cup (100 g) brown sugar

1 egg, room temperature

½ cup (115g) sour cream

1 teaspoon vanilla extract

¾ cup (180 ml) strong hot coffee

FROSTING

¾ cup (1½ sticks or 170 g) unsalted butter, room temperature

2 to 3 cups (400 to 600 g) powdered sugar

1 teaspoon vanilla extract

1 to 2 tablespoons instant strawberry gelatin mix (such as Jell-O)

1 to 2 tablespoons milk of choice

1. Preheat the oven to 350°F (175°C, or gas mark 4). Line 2 baking sheets with parchment paper.

2. In a large bowl, sift together the flour, cocoa powder, baking soda, and salt.

3. In a stand mixer bowl with a paddle attachment, cream the butter, sugar, and brown sugar for 3 minutes. Add the egg, sour cream, and vanilla. Mix until just combined.

4. Add one-third of the sifted ingredients and coffee to the butter mixture in separate additions, beginning and ending with the dry ingredients, stirring after each addition. (Example: Add one-third of the sifted ingredients, stir, add one-third of the coffee, stir, add remaining sifted ingredients, stir.) Continue alternating these ingredients until well combined.

5. Scoop 2½ tablespoons of the batter, spaced 2 to 3 inches (5 to 7.5 cm) apart, onto prepared baking sheets. Bake for 10 to 12 minutes, until the tops spring back when touched. The toothpick test for cake doneness will not work. Cool on baking sheets for 5 minutes and then transfer to a wire rack.

6. To make the frosting: In the stand mixer bowl with a whisk attachment, cream the butter for 3 minutes. On low, add 1 cup (200 g) powdered sugar. Mix until sugar is just incorporated, scrape down the bowl sides, then repeat with the remaining sugar. Add the vanilla, 1 tablespoon of gelatin mix, and 1 tablespoon of milk. Mix well, or until light and fluffy. Taste and add more gelatin or milk if needed. Spoon into a icing bag with a tip, or sandwich-size plastic bag with bottom corner cut off.

7. Pipe frosting on one cake round, top with a second.

8. Serve immediately or store wrapped in plastic in the refrigerator for up to a week.

Tell-Tale Lasagna Hearts

Behold these culinary creations inspired by Edgar Allan Poe's chilling tale of murder, guilt, and the beating of a hideous heart. A traditional symbol of love and affection, these hearts take on an anatomical look for a most gruesome main dish. May these layers of wonton wrapper, rich ricotta cheese filling, and tomato sauce entice those with feelings of great culpability to your table.

SPECIAL EQUIPMENT NEEDED

12-cup muffin pan

INGREDIENTS

2 tablespoons olive oil, or cooking oil spray

1 egg, beaten

1¾ cups (15 ounces) ricotta cheese

1¼ cups (10 ounces) frozen spinach, thawed and squeezed dry

½ cup (60 g) shredded Parmesan cheese

1 teaspoon garlic powder

1 teaspoon Italian seasoning

½ teaspoon onion powder

½ teaspoon salt

¼ teaspoon ground black pepper

4 cups (480 g) shredded mozzarella, divided

2 packages (12 ounces, or 340 g) square wonton wrappers

1 jar (24 ounces, or 680 g) garden-style pasta sauce

Minced fresh parsley, for topping (optional)

1. Preheat the oven to 375°F (190°C, or gas mark 5). Generously grease a 12-cup muffin pan with oil or cooking oil spray.

2. In a large bowl, mix the egg, ricotta cheese, spinach, Parmesan, garlic powder, Italian seasoning, onion powder, salt, pepper, and 1¼ cups (150 g) mozzarella.

3. Line each greased cup of the muffin pan with 1 wonton wrapper. Make sure to push down the wrapper around the bottom and sides of the muffin cup. Spoon 1 tablespoon of the ricotta mixture and ½ tablespoon of the pasta sauce into the cup. Top each with a second wonton wrapper, rotating the corners and pressing down at the center. Repeat layers as space allows: cheese mixture, pasta sauce, wonton wrapper. If needed, adjust the amount placed in each muffin cup. End with a wonton wrapper.

4. Sprinkle each lasagna heart with 1 to 2 teaspoons mozzarella cheese.

5. Bake for 20 to 25 minutes, until the cheese is melted and bubbly. Let cool in the pan for about 5 minutes. Once the muffin pan has cooled, the hearts should easily pop out. Assemble and bake the next round of lasagna hearts.

HEED: Only up for one batch of 12 lasagnas? After completing a muffin pan of lasagna hearts, stop and freeze the remaining cheese mixture in a zip-top plastic bag. Remove from the freezer, thaw, and proceed with wonton wrapper layering to make more hearts at a later date.

Ghostly Gourmet How-Tos

In this section, we delve deeper into the recipes featured in this book, providing extra ghoulish guidance and netherworld navigation on techniques and ingredients. You'll find devilishly detailed instructions on manifesting moons, baking bacon bows, tying life-like pumpkin rolls, and the many ways to pop popcorn. Refer to this section to confidently wield a knife on butternut squash or an unsuspecting orange. Create the most beautiful apparitions when you learn of the vast supernatural realm of decorative sprinkles and candy melts. Prepare to elevate your culinary know-how to ghostly greatness as you uncover the secrets of puff pastry. So grab your spectral spatula and prepare to haunt your cuisine to the next level.

How to Melt Candy Melts

Candy melts are a colored, flavored confectionery ingredient that's used for baking and decorating. They are specifically designed for easy melting and are commonly used for coating, dipping, and decorating baked goods (see recipes on pages 99, 104, 108, and 125). Here are two methods for melting candy melts. Choose the method that suits your preferences and the equipment you have available.

MICROWAVE METHOD

1. Add 1 cup (160 g) candy melts and 1 teaspoon vegetable shortening to a microwaveable bowl or sandwich-size plastic bag. Do not cover the bowl or close the bag.

2. Microwave on the defrost setting, or at 50 percent, for 1 minute. Stir thoroughly or knead the bag. This helps distribute the heat evenly and ensures that the melts melt uniformly. Continue to microwave at the same setting in 15- to 30-second intervals, stirring or kneading until candy is almost completely melted.

3. Candy melts should be smooth, free of lumps, and similar to the consistency of honey or syrup. If the mixture is still too thick, add an additional teaspoon of vegetable shortening and stir to combine.

STOVETOP METHOD

1. Use a double boiler, or create your own with a saucepan and medium heatproof bowl: Bring 2 to 3 cups (480 to 720 ml) water to a simmer in saucepan. Place a bowl on top of the saucepan, making sure the bottom of the bowl does not touch the simmering water. (Discard some of the water if necessary.)

2. Add 1 cup (160 g) candy melts and 1 tablespoon vegetable shortening to the heatproof bowl and stir.

3. Constantly stir the mixture until it melts into large chunks. Turn off the heat, remove the bowl from the saucepan, and continue to stir until the candy melts are smooth and free of lumps.

HEED: Avoid getting any water in contact with the candy melts, because it can cause them to harden and become unusable.

Be cautious not to overheat the candy melts, because this can cause them to become too thick or burn.

How to Create Phases of the Moon with Dough

Here is a simple way to recreate eight distinct phases of the moon using dough (see recipe on page 70).

1. With a rolling pin, roll the dough into eight 4 × 8 inches (10 × 20 cm) rectangles of uniform thickness.

2. A New Moon is invisible to the naked eye, so because the moon is an imperfect sphere, we will represent it here as a circle. Place the filling in a circle on the right side of a dough rectangle. Fold the dough in half. Use a large round cookie cutter or a knife and small bowl to cut the dough in a circle.

3. A Waxing Crescent Moon appears as a silver sliver moon, a curved shape that is wider in the middle than at its ends. It faces to the left in the Northern hemisphere. Place the filling in a thin crescent on the left side of a dough rectangle. Fold the dough in half. Use a knife to generously cut the dough into a banana shape.

4. A First Quarter Moon appears as a half circle in the night sky, but it is only a quarter of the way through its monthly journey. Place the filling in a semicircle on the left side of a dough rectangle. Fold the dough in half. Use a knife to generously cut the dough into a half disc. Make sure to leave plenty of dough around the edges to either roll or crimp by hand the pie closed.

5. A Waxing Gibbous Moon is a bright, more than half-lit, but not quite Full Moon. Place the filling in an almost circle on the left side of a dough rectangle. Fold the dough in half. Use a large round cookie cutter or a knife and small bowl to cut the dough into three-fourths of a circle.

6. A Full Moon is a fully illuminated disc when it is directly opposite the Sun and at a halfway point of its orbit. Place the filling in a circle on the right side of a dough rectangle. Fold the dough in half. Use a large round cookie cutter or a knife and small bowl to cut the dough in a circle.

7. A Waning Gibbous Moon is a bright, more than half-lit, but not quite Full Moon. Place the filling in an almost circle on the left side of a dough rectangle. Fold the dough in half. Use a large round cookie cutter or a knife and small bowl to cut the dough into three-fourths of a circle.

8. A Last Quarter Moon looks like a half circle. Place the filling in a semicircle on the right side of a dough rectangle. Fold the dough in half. Use a knife to generously cut the dough into a half disc. Make sure to leave plenty of dough around the edges to either roll or crimp by hand the pie closed.

9. A Waning Crescent Moon appears as a thin letter C. Place the filling in a thin crescent on the left side of a dough rectangle. Fold the dough in half. Use a knife to generously cut the dough into a banana shape. Seal all the dough edges by crimping with a fork or twisting to create a rope-like edge.

How to Find Your Way Around Decorative Sprinkles

In the bewitching world of sweet treats, decorative sprinkles and their brethren can cast a confounding spell of beauty and chaos. These tiny, colorful adornments are offered in a seemingly endless array of shapes and sizes. While each sprinkle holds its own sweet mysteries, let's pull back the curtain on the types of sprinkles used in *Creepy Kitchen*.

✳ **CANDY EYES:** Turn any treat into a face with candy eyes. Assorted sizes make stares small, medium, and large.

✳ **CONFETTI:** These round, flat sprinkles add a bright pop of color to desserts. They hold their shape and color well and add crunch to your confection.

✳ **NONPAREILS:** Nonpareils are teeny, tiny, ball-shaped sprinkles that are great for adding texture and overall decoration.

✳ **SPARKLING SUGAR:** This coarse-grained sugar has been dyed to look colorful and "sparkle" on baked goods. It is a larger crystal than table sugar and is best to use as an all-over dusting for a lustrous, crunchy finish to sweets.

✳ **SPRINKLE MIX:** Often the best way to add color and texture to your treats, the huge range of sprinkle mixes incorporates confetti, strands, nonpareils, and small candy shapes to meet your decorating needs.

✳ **SUGAR PEARLS:** Sugar pearls are small to medium-sized ball-shaped sprinkles with a shiny pearl or matte finish. They are hard and crunchy, so you do not want to use too many at once.

✳ **SUGAR STRANDS:** Also known as jimmies, sugar strands are long, thin, and crunchy. Their shape and color resist bleeding into frosting.

How to Create Foil Cylinders for Bacon Bows

To create a dimensional bow of bacon, you will need simple foil armatures to hold the meat in place while it's cooking.

TO CREATE TWO FOIL CYLINDERS

1. Cut a 24-inch (61-cm) long sheet of foil. Fold it in half lengthwise, then repeat twice more to create a 3-inch wide (7.5-cm) strip. Cut the 24-inch (61-cm) strip in half to yield two 12-inch (30.5-cm) sections.

2. Fold one 12-inch (30.5-cm) piece in half crosswise, and then fold it in half crosswise once more to make a thick 3-inch (7.5-cm) strip.

3. Roll the folded strip between your palms to form a cylindrical tube, securing the edges together with your fingers.

4. Repeat the same process with the other 12-inch (30.5-cm) piece of foil.

How to Supreme an Orange

"Supreming an orange" is a fancy way of saying you're going to peel and cut an orange into segments. This technique is an easy way to remove both the tough peel and the bitter pith quickly. Supremed oranges are perfect for salads, desserts, or garnishes.

1. To stabilize the orange, cut off the top and bottom of an unpeeled orange.

2. With a sharp knife, follow the contour of the fruit, removing the peel and white pith. The pith is the white tissue between the flesh and the peel.

3. Once peeled, identify the membranes separating the segments.

4. Slice alongside each membrane, releasing individual wedges. The result is a beautifully peeled and segmented orange.

How to Create Pumpkin Shapes for Your Dinner Rolls

If you're looking for a smoother, more realistic look to your pumpkin dinner rolls (see page 39), you've come to the right place. Here is a step-by-step guide to enjoying your dinner rolls the Halloween way.

1. Make a pumpkin shape on your dinner rolls by using cotton baking string. Measure about 24 inch (61 cm) of string, and wrap it around a dough ball like a ribbon on a present. Hold the middle of the string against the top of the dough ball, aligning it with the center.

2. Bring the string ends down, crossing them at the bottom. Twist the string once and bring the ends back up to the top of the dough ball, crossing them again at the center, creating a crisscross pattern. If you can, repeat to bring the string ends down to the bottom.

3. The roll will have 6 segments. Tie the string loosely and trim any excess string. The string does not need to be tight, as the dough will expand. Place the dough ball on a baking sheet, tie side down. Proceed with rising, egg wash, and baking as per the recipe.

4. Upon removing from the oven, let cool for several minutes. Carefully cut the string as needed to remove it from the roll. Go slowly and be mindful of the dough that has baked over the string.

How to Peel a Butternut Squash

Peeling and deseeding a butternut squash can be a bit tricky due to its tough skin. Remember to exercise caution to keep the squash from slipping and be mindful of your fingers while handling. Here's a step-by-step tutorial:

1. Cut off the top stem of the butternut squash using a sharp knife.

2. Slice off a small portion from the bottom to create a stable base.

3. With a vegetable peeler or a sharp knife, peel off the squash skin. Make long, downward strokes, following the contour of the squash. Be cautious because the skin can be tough.

4. Once the squash is peeled, it's time to deseed it. Slice the squash in half lengthwise, separating the narrower neck portion from the bottom portion.

5. Flip the squash over and use a spoon or scoop to scrape out the seeds and pulp in both halves.

6. Flip the squash back over so it is cut side down and stable. Cut into cubes.

How to Pop Popcorn

Here are two different methods for popping your popcorn (see recipe on page 95). You can do what you feel the most comfortable with; there is no wrong or right way to do this.

MICROWAVE METHOD

1. Pour the popcorn kernels into a large microwaveable bowl. Cover with a microwave-safe ceramic dinner plate to act as a lid.

2. Place the popcorn in the microwave, set the cooking time, and cook on high heat. Typically, it takes about 2 to 4 minutes, depending on your microwave's wattage.

3. You will hear the kernels popping. Continue to monitor the process to prevent burning.

4. Once the popping slows down to a few seconds between pops, remove the bowl immediately. Be cautious as it will be hot.

5. Carefully remove the cover with potholders, opening it away from you to avoid steam burns. Transfer the popcorn to large bowl.

STOVETOP METHOD

1. In a large, heavy-bottomed pot with a tight-fitting lid over medium-high heat, add 2 to 3 tablespoons vegetable oil.

2. Once hot, add the popcorn kernels to the pot and swirl gently to coat the kernels with oil.

3. Cover the pot with the lid, leaving it slightly ajar to let steam escape. This will prevent the popcorn from becoming soggy.

4. As the pot heats up, listen for popping sounds. Using potholders and making sure lid is secure, shake the pot occasionally to prevent burning.

5. Once the popping slows down to a few seconds between pops, remove the pot from the heat. Keep the lid on for a moment to allow any remaining kernels to pop.

6. Carefully remove the lid, opening it away from you to avoid steam burns. Transfer the freshly popped popcorn to large bowl. Remove any unpopped kernels.

How to Make Chilling Cheddar Puff Pastries

Grilled cheese sandwiches are great and everything, but have you ever had a Cheddar Puff Pastry? This flaky, tangy, and nutty delight makes for a frightfully delicious feast when served along with Attack of the Killer Tomato Soup (see page 66), or as a savory breakfast treat.

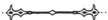

SPECIAL EQUIPMENT NEEDED

Pastry brush

INGREDIENTS

2 tablespoons unsalted butter

4 or 5 large shallots, thickly sliced

¼ teaspoon salt, or to taste

1 to 2 tablespoons all-purpose flour, for dusting

1 package puff pastry sheets (two sheets per box), thawed

¾ cup (170 g) extra-sharp Cheddar cheese, sliced thin

1 egg, beaten, for egg wash

1. In a small skillet over medium heat, melt the butter. Add the shallots, sprinkle with salt and stir. Cook for 9 to 12 minutes, until browned and caramelized. Set aside.

2. Preheat the oven to 400°F (205°C, or gas mark 6). Line a baking sheet with parchment paper.

3. Unfold one sheet of pastry onto lightly floured parchment paper. If the pastry cracks, wet fingers and press the edges of the crack together. Cut the pastry into thirds along the fold lines. Cut each third in half.

4. On the baking sheet, make 6 small groups of caramelized shallots. Layer 2 slices of cheese on top of each. Carefully place pastry rectangles over the cheese. Evenly press down to adhere the cheese and shallots to the pastry. (Pastry and cheese will expand and melt while baking, so leave room between each pastry.) Use a fork or your fingers to crimp and seal the edges of pastry dough to the parchment paper.

5. In a small bowl, whisk the egg for the egg wash. Using a pastry brush, apply a thin layer of egg on each pastry rectangle.

6. Bake for 10 to 25 minutes, until the pastry is golden and flakey. After 10 minutes, check often to prevent burning. Let cool for 5 to 10 minutes. Gently flip the pastries with a spatula.

7. Serve warm and enjoy!

Index

Acknowledgments

This project would not have been possible without the support of many people.

To Brian, thank you for being my partner in all things eerie. Your willingness to taste-test recipes and your boundless patience during this creepy adventure has been invaluable. You are my secret ingredient.

I want to express my heartfelt thanks to two very special individuals who are also my Halloween Helpers: Max and Ruby.

Max, your insightful feedback, tips on garnishes, and Spicy Creepy Crema recipe summoned something extraordinary into this book. Ruby, your extra-terrestrial excitement for devouring snacks and desserts, assistance in perfectly placing those eyeballs, and frequent costume changes brought so much joy to me and to every recipe.

Thank you to my Mom and Dad for your support. The family recipes, vintage Halloween clippings and books, and childhood mementos you shared brought back wonderful memories. I still think about that awesome witch costume you made me when I was five.

My deepest gratitude goes to RK, who provided opportunity, belief, and pep-talks throughout this process.

I am also grateful to: Karel Traister for sharing her cooking expertise, presentation perspectives, and enlightening explanation of how macaroni and cheese is not a main course; Lisa Conn and the Marchiafava family for sharing your knowlege of pork roasts and meatloaf; Eli Vandenberg for thoughts on dips, and missed meat dates; Dana Sachs for taste-testing and wonderfully honest recipe feedback; Linda and Frank Kall for your enduring warmth and for generously sharing your slow cooker recipes; Mike and Matt's Italian Market for advice on what antipasto makes the best edible eyeballs; and of course, mystical meowzers Nacho and Flash.

About the Author

Based in South Philadelphia, Pennsylvania, **Kim Kindelsperger** is a creative, crafty individual with an eye for the unusual. She finds joy in the art of cooking and has a deep affection for cats. Kim's offbeat and idiosyncratic nature is reflected in her unique creations, including dinner her children will actually eat, yarn bombs, sweaters for cats, and various paper crafts. With a strong community focus, she actively engages in her neighborhood and public schools.

About the Illustrator

Kitty Willow Wilson, an artist working in picturesque Somerset, UK, draws inspiration from the ethereal realm of ghosts, the untamed spirit of animals and plants, and the timeless allure of Victorian aesthetics. In a delicate dance between light and darkness, whimsical and spooky, her artwork features an array of enchanting creatures from this world and beyond. Through these visual wonderlands, she invites you to embrace the beauty that lies within the shadows of the natural world.

First published in 2024 by Rock Point, an imprint of The Quarto Group,
142 West 36th Street, 4th Floor, New York, NY 10018, USA
(212) 779-4972 www.Quarto.com

10 9 8 7 6 5 4 3 2 1

ISBN: 978-1-63106-989-5

Digital edition published in 2024
eISBN: 978-0-7603-8763-4

Library of Congress Cataloging-in-Publication Data

Names: Kindelsperger, Kim, author.
Title: Creepy kitchen : 60 terror-rific recipes that'll possess your
   palette / Kim Kindelsperger.
Description: New York, NY, USA : Rock Point, an imprint of The Quarto
   Group, 2024. | Includes index. | Summary: "The 60 spooky foods included
   in the Creepy Kitchen cookbook are perfect for the ghoul at heart"–
   Provided by publisher.
Identifiers: LCCN 2024002577 (print) | LCCN 2024002578 (ebook) | ISBN
   9781631069895 (hardcover) | ISBN 9780760387634 (ebook)
Subjects: LCSH: Cooking. | LCGFT: Cookbooks.
Classification: LCC TX714 .K563 2024 (print) | LCC TX714 (ebook) | DDC
   641.5–dc23/eng/20240126
LC record available at https://lccn.loc.gov/2024002577
LC ebook record available at https://lccn.loc.gov/2024002578

Group Publisher: Rage Kindelsperger
Editorial Director: Erin Canning
Creative Director: Laura Drew
Managing Editor: Cara Donaldson
Editor: Keyla Pizarro-Hernández
Editorial Assistant: Tobiah Agurkis
Illustrations: Kitty Willow Wilson
Interior Design: Laura Klynstra

Printed in China